# SING TO THE LORD
# A New Song

*A New Moravian Songbook*

Collected and edited by
The Moravian Music Foundation

**Moravian Church in America**
Bethlehem, Pennsylvania
Winston-Salem, North Carolina

**Sing to the Lord a New Song: A New Moravian Songbook**

Moravian Music Foundation
457 S. Church St.
Winston-Salem, NC 27101
Info@moravianmusic.org

Interprovincial Board of Communication
1021 Center St., PO Box 1245
Bethlehem, PA 18018
pubs@mcnp.org

Music Typography: Moravian Music Foundation
Cover Illustration © Mike Riess, IBOC

Printed in the U.S.A. by McNaughton & Gunn, Saline, Michigan
Third Printing: March 2016

ISBN: 978-1-933571-45-4

FSC
www.fsc.org
MIX
Paper from
responsible sources
FSC® C011935

# PREFACE

The Christian church has been blessed with a marvelous flowering of creativity in song during the past 30 years. While these new songs cannot, and should not, replace rich musical traditions, each generation is called to find new expressions of faith, love and hope. A constantly changing world calls for different images for God, expressions of Christian community and challenges for Christian ministry and service.

*Sing to the Lord a New Song: A New Moravian Songbook* is an outgrowth of this fruitfulness in the Moravian Church in America. More than 350 submissions were reviewed to produce this collection intended for congregational worship. The collection includes songs and hymns by 51 contemporary text-writers and composers, lay and clergy, young and not-so-young, from all regions of the Moravian Church in North America. There are surely many other poets and composers at work in the Moravian Church. Our hope is that this collection will inspire them to share their work or encourage others to try their hand at writing a congregational song.

Like many of the hymnals of the ancient Unity, this collection is arranged according to the "essentials" as defined by Luke of Prague. On the part of God: the good will of God, the saving work of Christ, and the gifts of the Holy Spirit. On the part of humanity: faith, love, and hope. Then come hymns on "ministerials" -- the church and sacraments -- followed by hymns on mission and life in Christ.

Each song can be accompanied on keyboard and/or guitar; other instruments may be added to enrich the musical experience. We rejoice at the diversity of the musical styles of these songs, at the varied images and expressions of faith, and yet at the consistency with deep-rooted Moravian Christ-centered faith, love and hope. The liturgical materials are not intended to be all-inclusive, but rather to add to those already available.

This preface concludes as the prefaces of every Moravian hymnal have since 1789, with the following words:

*May all who use these hymns experience at all times the blessed effects of complying with the Apostle Paul's injunction in Ephesians 5:18-19, "Be filled with the Spirit, as you sing psalms and hymns and spiritual songs among yourselves, singing and making melody to the Lord in your hearts." Yea, may they anticipate, while here below, though in a humble and imperfect strain, the song of the blessed above, who, being redeemed out of every kindred, and tongue, and people, and nation, and having washed their robes, and made them white in the blood of the Lamb, are standing before the throne, and singing in perfect harmony with the many angels round about it, "Worthy is the Lamb that was slain, to receive power, and riches, and wisdom, and strength, and honor, and glory, and blessing, for ever and ever. Amen!"*

# SING TO THE LORD A NEW SONG:
# A New Moravian Songbook
## CONTENTS

# LITURGY OF SERVANTHOOD

O Lord, our God, your wisdom and power are beyond our comprehension. Yet our hearts know you intimately.

**Our love for you and our awe of you join together in our praise to your holy name.**

You are the one we turn to when we hear your invitation to be your disciples; when we feel the call to servanthood.

**You, O Lord, provide strength and wisdom for each day and hope for the journey.**

It is by faith in you that we respond to your call to serve.

**We believe that you are our source of love and provide the resources for loving.**
**We believe that you redeem not only our lives but also our actions so that our small human offerings have divine results.**
**We believe that your Spirit empowers us to be all that you created us to be for your purpose.**

CASSEL (167 A), hymn 84

Holy God of all creation, give us vision, love and nerve
to respond to our first calling on this earth to care and serve.
Show the world by our example how to live each waking hour,
as we strive to humbly follow, sharing your creative power.

© IBOC/MMF

Yet the call to serve can, at times, be overwhelming. The need before us is more than one person can handle alone.

**We thank you, Lord, for calling us to work as one body. Your Body is made manifest in us as we work together to serve your children.**

Lord, many people in our community show your love through their actions.

**They shelter the homeless. They feed the hungry. They accompany the elderly. They champion the battle with mental illness. They help others become better parents. They donate their blood, their sweat, and their personal belongings.**

Lord, many people in our church generously offer their lives to your service.

**They teach your word. They visit the sick and home-bound. They provide fellowship for our church family. They serve as leaders and decision makers. They make worship a meaningful experience. They support our ministry in prayer.**

1

Let us identify the organizations in our church and community that make up the tangible Body of Christ.

(Speak aloud the names of church and community groups that provide loving service.)

3

Lord, we thank you for these people whom you have joined together for your purpose.

**We thank you for people who live what they believe and believe what they live. We thank you for the Spirit of Christ which dwells in such people in our church and community.**

By your grace, Lord, we stand among those who will hear you say, "I was hungry and you gave me food, I was thirsty and you gave me something to drink, I was a stranger and you welcomed me, I was naked and you clothed me, sick and you cared for me, in prison and you visited me."

**And we will say, "Lord, when did we see you hungry, or thirsty, or a stranger, or naked or in prison?"**

And you will assure us, Lord, with your words, "Just as you have done it to one of the least of these who are members of my family, you did it to me."

CHALLENGE, Hymn 74

Into the world Christ Jesus sends us,
to love like he loved wherever we go:
just down the street, into the cities,
crossing the borders of culture as though
nothing, but nothing, could keep us away –
this is the challenge of our mission.

Into the world Christ Jesus sends us
to make disciples wherever we go:
teaching his truth, seeking commitment,
welcoming strangers and watching them grow.
Warming cold hearts with the flames of God's love –
this is the challenge of our mission.

# THE GOOD SHEPHERD

Jesus Christ is the Good Shepherd, foretold by prophets, priests and kings. He was destined to be a ruler who is to shepherd my people Israel. (Matt. 2:3-6)

**As our Good Shepherd, he gave his life for the sake of his sheep and made a way for us to enter his pastures in peace.**

HAYN (82 D)

Je - sus makes my heart re - joice, I'm his sheep and know his voice; he's a Shep-herd, kind and gra-cious, and his pas - tures are de - li - cious; con - stant love to me he shows, yea, my ver - y name he knows.

As the Good Shepherd, Jesus lays down his life for the sheep. A hireling, who does not know the sheep, will run away if a wolf comes close. The hired hand does not care for the sheep.

**The Good Shepherd knows his sheep, as only a shepherd can. He calls his sheep by name and welcomes them into his pasture.**

The Good Shepherd has made us whole by the blood of an eternal covenant. He has made us complete in everything good so that we may do his will, working among us that which is pleasing in his sight.

**May the God of peace, who brought back from the dead our Lord Jesus, the great shepherd of the sheep, keep us close to him.** (Heb. 13:20-21)

**Lord Jesus Christ, we pray now for all who confess you as Lord and Savior. There are many sheep but only one Shepherd. For all who call upon the name of the Lord will be saved. We pray as well for all those who are still far away from God's saving power:**
> **for those who have strayed from the flock;**
> **for those who are confused and distracted by falsehoods;**
> **for all who are close to us in faith and heritage;**
> **and for all who have never heard the name of Jesus, our Good Shepherd.**
**We pray for their salvation that comes from profession and confidence in the strong saving name of our Lord, Jesus Christ. Amen.**

He will feed his flock like a shepherd.

**He will gather the lambs in his arms and carry them in his bosom, and gently lead the mother sheep.** (Matthew 25, Isaiah 40)

SHEPHERD (MBW 731)

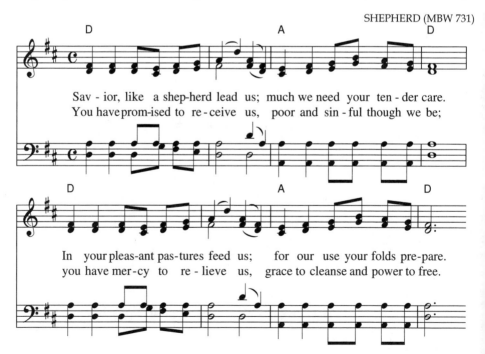

Sav - ior, like a shep-herd lead us; much we need your ten - der care.
You have prom-ised to re - ceive us, poor and sin - ful though we be;

In your pleas-ant pas-tures feed us; for our use your folds pre-pare.
you have mer-cy to re - lieve us, grace to cleanse and power to free.

Bless-ed Je-sus, bless-ed Je-sus, you have bought us, yours we are.
Bless-ed Je-sus, bless-ed Je-sus, you have loved us, love us still.

Bless-ed Je-sus, bless-ed Je-sus, you have bought us, yours we are.
Bless-ed Je-sus, bless-ed Je-sus, you have loved us, love us still.

And when the Chief Shepherd appears, you will win the crown of glory that never fades away.

**Grace, mercy and peace will follow us all the days of our lives.**

# EXAMINE PRAYER

God of peace, we seek your peace in our hearts and in our world.

> We celebrate your serenity of spirit in the midst of life's opportunities and challenges. We celebrate harmony in our families and in all our relationships. We celebrate the days when our families live in your peace without fear.

Yet we confess that, at times, we act in ways that do not support the spiritual life we celebrate.

> At times our response to life is less than serene. At times we contribute to the conflict within our families and relationships. At times our actions or attitudes do not provide a safe place for others to grow. At times, Lord God, our hearts do not glorify you.

*Reflect on the recent past. What, in your life, do you celebrate?*
*For what are you thankful?*

"And they shall stand every morning, thanking and praising the Lord."

(1 Chronicles 23:20)

> **"To you, O God, I give thanks and praise, for you have given me wisdom and power."**
> (Daniel 2:23)

*Reflect on the recent past. Where have you witnessed God's presence in your life?*

"Lord, where can I go from your Spirit? If I ascend to heaven or make my bed in Sheol, you are there."

(Psalm 139: 7-8)

> **Jesus assures us, "I will be with you always to the end of the age."**
> (Matthew 28:20)

*Reflect on the recent past. What might you have done differently to glorify God?*

"You, O Lord, are good and forgiving, abounding in steadfast love to all who call on you."

(Psalm 86: 5)

> **"Give ear, O Lord, to my prayer; listen to my cry of supplication. In the day of my trouble I call on you, for you will answer me."**
> (Psalm 86:6-7)

God of peace, we seek your peace in our hearts and in our world. With grateful hearts we give thanks to you. Fill us with your Spirit. Renew our lives with your purpose. Open our hearts to your will.

"Bless the Lord, O my soul, and do not forget all his benefits – who forgives all your iniquity, who heals all your diseases, who redeems your life from the Pit, who crowns you with steadfast love and mercy, who satisfies you with good as long as you live so that your youth is renewed like the eagle's." Amen. (Psalm 103:2-5)

# REFLECTIONS ON PSALM 121

I lift up my eyes to the hills - from where will my help come?

**My help comes from the Lord, who made heaven and earth.**

*Silent reflection: How ready and willing am I to rely on the Lord's help? Where, in my life, might I rely more on God?*

He will not let your foot be moved; he who keeps you will not slumber.

**He who keeps Israel will neither slumber nor sleep.**

*Silent reflection: How have I experienced God's attentiveness in my life?*

The Lord is your keeper; the Lord is your shade at your right hand.

**The sun shall not strike you by day, nor the moon by night.**

*Silent reflection: In what way am I feeling the heat of daily living? What do I need to say to God about this?*

The Lord will keep you from all evil; he will keep your life.

**The Lord will keep your going out and your coming in from this time on and forevermore.**

*Silent reflection: What tempts me to live in ways that are not consistent with God? What do I have to say to God about this? How does God respond?*

TALLIS CANON (22 T, hymn 64)

We humbly gather in this place
to praise you, Lord, and seek your grace,
and, Holy Spirit, we now pray:
come, work among us every day.

As we go forth to do your will,
Lord, guide us and your word fulfill,
and show us how to work and be
your blest disciples, wholly free.

© 2006 by John Craver

# A Journey Through Psalm 23

The Lord is my shepherd, I shall not want.

> **I want so much, Lord. I desire so many things that promise to make my life easier, fuller or more exciting and meaningful. And yet the "things" of this life do not provide the fullness of life. Give me wisdom to know my wants from my needs. Give me eyes to see the fullness of my life in you. Give me a heart that is willing to journey with the Shepherd.**

He makes me lie down in green pastures.

> **Because of you, Lord, my life is fertile. You planted the seed of faith in my heart and you cause it to grow. Everything in my life — the joys, the sorrows, the worries, the discoveries — has been embraced by your love and contributes to who I am today.**

He leads me beside still waters.

> **Although there is turbulence in life, your spirit fills me with peace and calm. There is a stillness that you provide when I find myself navigating troubled waters. Protect me from fear, worry and anger when life becomes threatening, that I might enjoy life as you intended it.**

He restores my soul.

> **Lord, when circumstances of life threaten to defeat me, you offer healing to me. Even if I question your presence in my life or if worry overwhelms me and I wonder if I can go on, you refresh my soul. In time, you breathe new life into me. You fill me with so much of yourself that the world simply becomes the place where I come to know you.**

He leads me in right paths for his name's sake.

> **When I look back at my life and see the choices that I have made, I stand humbled and acknowledge your guidance. I seek your wisdom as I face each day. I ask that you journey with me one step at a time.**

Even though I walk through the darkest valley I fear no evil for you are with me; your rod and your staff – they comfort me.

> **Challenges will come. They will threaten to take my breath away. But your breath remains. Your Spirit guards my life. You give me hope. You give me peace and the warmth of your Son brings a smile to my heart.**

You prepare a table before me in the presence of my enemies.

> You have invited me to a party in your honor. There is a place for me at your table, in your kingdom. With all the faithful, Lord, you have welcomed me to break bread with you and confess my faith in your love. Those who ridiculed me because of my faith will see your glory in me. Let them see it now so that they might take their place at your table also.

You anoint my head with oil.

> You have chosen me, Lord, for a holy purpose. You have gifted me to perform your work. You have called me to do your will. Convict me with your Spirit so that I might never betray you and assure me of your forgiveness in the event that I do.

My cup overflows.

> The words of my mouth are attempts to express what cannot be spoken. My life is so full, so rich that only my heart can sing the praise that you deserve. In my greatest moments of emptiness, Lord, you fill me up. Fill me now with your truth, your Word.

Surely goodness and mercy shall follow me all the days of my life.

> It doesn't matter where I live, where I work, where I travel, who I am with or how long I walk this earth. If I bring you with me, my journey will be blessed.

And I shall dwell in the house of the Lord my whole life long.

> May my life be a prayer. May my life be a witness. May my life be my confession of faith in you, Lord Jesus Christ. Amen.

# Mothers' Day

Lord, on this day set aside to honor and remember mothers, we give you thanks for our mothers. We are grateful that you chose to give us life through them, and that they received the gift of life from your hands, and gave it to us. Thank you for the sacrifices they made in carrying us and giving us birth.

We thank you for the women who raised us, who were our mothers in childhood. Whether birth mom, adopted mom, older sister, aunt, grandmother, stepmother or someone else, we thank you for those women who held us and fed us, who cared for us and kissed away our pain. We pray that our lives may reflect the love they showed us, and that they would be pleased to be called our moms.

We pray for older moms whose children are grown.

**Grant them joy and satisfaction for a job well done.**

We pray for new moms experiencing changes they could not predict.

**Grant them rest and peace as they trust you for the future.**

We pray for pregnant women who will soon be moms.

**Grant them patience and good counsel in the coming months.**

We pray for moms who face the demands of single parenthood.

**Grant them strength and wisdom.**

We pray for moms who enjoy financial abundance.

**Grant them time to share with their families.**

We pray for moms who are raising their children in poverty.

**Grant them relief and justice.**

We pray for moms who try to balance vocation and family.

**Grant them courage for the living of each day.**

We pray for stepmoms.

**Grant them patience and understanding and love.**

We pray for moms who are separated from their children.

**Grant them faith and hope.**

We pray for moms in marriages that are in crisis.

**Grant them support and insight.**

We pray for moms who have lost children.

**Grant them comfort in the resurrection of Jesus Christ.**

We pray for mothers who aborted their children.

**Grant them healing and peace.**

We pray for moms who gave up their children for adoption.

**Grant them peace and confidence as they trust in your providence.**

We pray for adoptive mothers.

**Grant them joy and gratitude for the gift you have provided.**

We pray for girls and women who think about being moms.

**Grant them wisdom and discernment.**

We pray for women who desperately want, or wanted, to be moms.

**Grant them grace to accept your timing and will.**

We pray for all women who have assumed the mother's role in a child's life.

**Grant them joy and the appreciation of others.**

We pray for moms who show us the way of faith.

**Grant them the guidance of the Holy Spirit.**

We pray for those people present who are grieving the loss of their mother in the past year.

**Grant them comfort and hope in Christ's resurrection.**

*(All women and girls are invited to stand for a blessing.)*

Lord, we thank you for the gift of motherhood. We thank you for the many examples of faithful mothers in scripture, like Sarah, Hannah, Elizabeth, and Lois. Now hear the names of other women who have inspired us by their motherly examples . . .

We are mindful this day of all these women, and especially Mary the mother of our Lord Jesus Christ, who had the courage in faith to say "yes" to your calling. May these women gathered here today emulate these examples of faith. And may they model for all the rest of us what it means to be your disciple. Bless them on this special day; in the name of Jesus Christ.

**Amen.**

# FATHERS' DAY

Lord, on this day set aside to honor and remember fathers, we give you thanks for our fathers. We are grateful that you chose to give us life through them, and that they received the gift of life from your hands, and gave it to us. Thank you for the sacrifices they made in the form of time, courage and patience.

We thank you for the men who raised us, who were our fathers in childhood. Whether biological father, adopted dad, older brother, uncle, grandfather, stepfather or someone else, we thank you for those men who guided and protected us, who cared for us and held us in your love. We pray that our lives may reflect the love they showed us, and that they would be pleased to be called our dads.

We pray for older dads whose children are grown.

**Grant them joy and satisfaction for a job well done.**

We pray for new dads experiencing changes they could not predict.

**Grant them rest and peace as they trust you for the future.**

We pray for expectant men who will soon be dads.

**Grant them patience and good counsel in the coming months.**

We pray for dads who face the demands of single parenthood.

**Grant them strength and wisdom.**

We pray for dads who enjoy financial abundance.

**Grant them time to share with their families.**

We pray for dads who are raising their children in poverty.

**Grant them relief and justice.**

We pray for dads who try to balance vocation and family.

**Grant them courage for the living of each day.**

We pray for stepdads.

**Grant them patience and understanding and love.**

We pray for dads who are separated from their children.

**Grant them faith and hope.**

We pray for dads in marriages that are in crisis.

**Grant them support and insight.**

We pray for dads who have lost children.

**Grant them comfort in the resurrection of Jesus Christ.**

We pray for fathers whose children's lives ended in abortion.

**Grant them healing and peace.**

We pray for dads who gave up their children for adoption.

**Grant them peace and confidence as they trust in your providence.**

We pray for adoptive fathers.

**Grant them joy and gratitude for the gift you have provided.**

We pray for boys and men who think about being dads.

**Grant them wisdom and discernment.**

We pray for men who desperately want, or wanted, to be dads.

**Grant them grace to accept your timing and will.**

We pray for all men who have assumed the father's role in a child's life.

**Grant them joy and the appreciation of others.**

We pray for dads who show us the way of faith.

**Grant them the guidance of the Holy Spirit.**

We pray for those people present who are grieving the loss of their father in the past year.

**Grant them comfort and hope in Christ's resurrection.**

*(All men and boys are invited to stand for a blessing.)*

Lord, we thank you for the gift of fatherhood. We thank you for the many examples of faithful fathers in scripture, like Abraham, Isaac, Jacob and Zechariah. Now hear the names of other men who have inspired us by their fatherly examples . . .

We are mindful this day of all these men, and especially Joseph the earthly father of our Lord Jesus Christ, who had the courage in faith to say "yes" to your calling. May these men and boys gathered here today emulate these examples of faith. And may they model for all the rest of us what it means to be your disciple. Bless them on this special day; in the name of Jesus Christ.

**Amen.**

# inTending commUnity
## A Reflection

You spoke, Lord God, and *it was so.*
You saw that what was – was good!

There must have been something about Light that pleased you.
Something to the ordering of Sun, Moon and Stars
making you smile.

Something in the Dance of Life across the sky,
through the waters and across the ground
returning your blessing to you.

What then, Lord, did you see and say, "It is not good"?
*That the man should be alone.*
How is it, Holy Spirit, Voice and Vision,
that two are better than one?
*For if they fall, one will lift up the other.*

Why, Beloved Son of our Father in heaven,
are the "greatest" commandments hardly breakable
apart from the living presence of community
(human and divine)?

Wherever two or more are together in your name –
Where the needs of the very least
reveal the presence of the Most High –

The Love that you are and the Life that you give
leave little room for faith that *is not* a gathering
and a sharing of heart and soul and strength.


© by Brian Dixon

# A New Psalm to the Lord Now Sing 17

1. A new psalm to the Lord now sing, a
2. When foes without and fears with-in and
3. Praise Je-sus Christ, our Pas-chal Lamb, who
4. For-give our sins, our souls re-pair by

song of thanks and praise, for mer-cies be-yond
cares up-on us weigh, God, who our strength and
gave his life for us; to-geth-er let us
your re-deem-ing grace; by faith we'll walk and

num-ber-ing and cour-age for these days.
shield has been, will help us still to-day.
fol-low him, and with him bear the cross.
work and share un-til we see your face.

5. Give us your Holy Spirit, Lord;
we would disciples be,
and know, as we obey your word,
the truth that makes us free.

6. Eternal Father, Spirit, Son,
our Maker, Guide, and Friend,
help us to say, "Your will be done,"
and serve you to the end.

TEXT: Carl Helmich, Jr. (2010). © 2013 by Interprovincial Board of Communication
and Moravian Music Foundation
TUNE: Alexander Robert Reinagle (1836)

C.M.

ST. PETER (14 T)

# 18     Dear Christ, in Faith

1 Dear Christ, in faith we heard your call in this and ev-'ry
2 O Lord, in love you came to earth to rise, but first to
3 And so, good Sav-ior, now we pray: grant us your Spir-it's

land, the Gos-pel to pro-claim to all, up-held by your strong
die; yet in your death we find our birth, all lives to sanc-ti-
pow'r as in the past, so in our day and ev-'ry fu-ture

hand. At times our steps have not been sure, but
fy. When all your sav-ing works we view, our
hour: with hope may our lives tes-ti-fy that

TEXT: C. Daniel Crews (1999). © 2013 by Interprovincial Board of Communication and Moravian Music Foundation
TUNE: Herrnhut (c. 1740); C. Gregor *Choralbuch* (1784)

8.6.8.6.8.8.8.6. Iambic

WORSHIP (159 A)

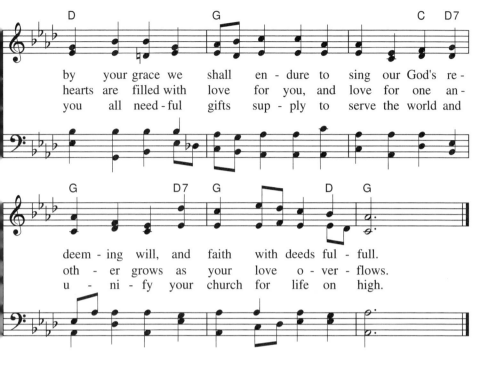

by          your grace we        shall        en - dure to        sing   our God's re -
hearts   are    filled with      love         for    you,    and    love  for   one   an -
you        all     need - ful      gifts         sup - ply   to      serve  the world and

deem - ing   will,   and      faith       with deeds ful - full.
oth  -  er   grows   as       your        love    o - ver - flows.
u   -    ni - fy   your      church    for      life    on     high.

*The following verse may be used for anniversary occasions:*

Our Savior, many years ago
you brought us to this place,
and still we seek to learn and grow
to manifest your grace.
With wider vision may we give
ourselves to others while we live;
O may we all with one accord
still follow you, dear Lord.

# 19 Lost Am I From God My Maker

1. Lost am I from God my Mak - er, lost in dark - ness and des - pair, like a coin dropped from a pock - et in a cor - ner, un - der chair.
2. Could God care e - nough to find me, light a lan - tern, sweep the floor, like a care - ful wom - an look - ing in each cor - ner, by each door?
3. Search - ing ev - er now she sees me where I lie for - got - ten, tossed; pulls me out in - to the sun - light where I shine, no long - er lost.
4. With de - light and joy - ful won - der she re - joic - es o - ver me. Calls her friends, "Come, cel - e - brate now one, once lost, who now is free."

TEXT: M. Lynnette Delbridge. © 2010 by M. Lynnette Delbridge
TUNE: John Goss (1869)

8.7.8.7.
LAUDA ANIMA (PRAISE MY SOU

|        |       |        |       |      |     |       |      |
|--------|-------|--------|-------|------|-----|-------|------|
| Will   | God   | seek   | me?   | Will | God | find  | me?  |
| Will   | God   | seek   | me?   | Will | God | find  | me?  |
| God    | has   | sought | me!   | God  | has | found | me,  |
| God    | has   | sought | me!   | God  | has | found | me!  |

|        |       |      |      |      |      |       |
|--------|-------|------|------|------|------|-------|
| or     | long  | si - | lence | must | I   | bear? |
| Can    | my    | heart | with | hope | now | soar? |
| car -  | ing   | nev - | er   | what | the | cost. |
| God's  | per - | sis - | tent | love | the | key.  |

5.   Grateful that God dared to rescue
     me from dusty, deep despair,
     joyful I go where God leads me,
     bold good news and call to share.
     God has sought us! God has found us!
     Live God's love, a gift so rare.

# 20     God Is Our Refuge

1. God is our ref - uge, strength, and home, our help and peace to - day. Though pow'rs may fail and sor - rows come, God's light will show the way.

2. Be still and know our Lord is God, whose love at - tends our prayers. Each whis - pered word, each si - lent hope finds com - fort in God's care.

TEXT: Willie Israel (2010). © 2013 by Interprovincial Board of Communication
and Moravian Music Foundation
TUNE: Traditional, from *A Sett of Tunes* (1720)

C.I

MEA

# How Big Is God?

*Invite children for suggestions of things God is bigger than, and sing again!*

TEXT and MUSIC: source unknown.

## 22  Praise, My Soul, the King of Heaven

1. Praise, my soul, the King ____ of heav - en, ___ to his feet  your trib -
2. Ten - der-ly ___ he shields ____ and spares us, ___ well our fee - ble frame

____ ute bring. ___     Ran-somed, healed, re - stored, for - giv - en,
___ he knows,        in   his hands he  gen - tly  bears us,

TEXT: Henry Francis Lyte (1834), alt.
TUNE: Steve Gray (2011). © 2011 by Steve Gray

THE GOOD WILL OF GOD

King! _____ Praise him for his grace
flows. _____ An - gels help us to _____

_ and fa - vor to his peo - ple in ____ dis - tress.
_ a - dore him, who be-hold him face _____ to face.

Praise him, still the same ____ for - ev - er, ___ slow to chide and swift
Sun and moon bow down ____ be - fore him, all who dwell in time

# 23 God Meets Us Where We Are

Capo 2: G — C — G

1. God meets us where we are; God
2. God meets us where we are, if
3. God meets us where we are: our
4. God meets us where we are; O

C — A7 — D — G — C

comes to bring us grace. God comes to make one
we but turn God's way to see our-selves in
doubts, re - grets, and fears. God comes to com - fort,
may I there-fore see as I em - brace God's

Am — A7 — D — C — D — G

fam - i - ly of the whole hu - man race.
need of grace, just as the world to - day.
re - as - sure, and dry our an - guished tears.
chil - dren's needs, God has a place for me.

TEXT: Robert Rominger (2008) © 2008 by R. L. Rominger, III
TUNE: William H. Walter (1825-1893)

S.M.
FESTAL SONG (582 X)

# Rejoice, All Those in Christ's Command 24

TEXT: Zachariah D. Bailey (2009)
TUNE: Zachariah D. Bailey (2009)
© 2009 by Zachariah D. Bailey

8.6.8.6.D.

**25**

# Great Sabbath Hymn
## (The Grave Today Is Holding)

1. The grave to-day is hold - ing our Lord, our life, our love;
2. Your Sab - bath rest, dear Sav - ior, we cel - e - brate with joy;

with - in its depths en - fold - ing the heights of heav'n a - bove.
to praise its sol - emn splen - dor our high - est gifts em-ploy.

In death, most gra-cious Sav - ior, you proved our dear - est Friend,
Lead us to rise vic - to - rious as you burst bonds of hell,

the on - ly path which leads us to life which knows no end.
to join in hymns most glo - rious your sav - ing power to tell.

TEXT: C. Daniel Crews (1995). © 2013 by Interprovincial Board of Communication       7.6.7.6.D. Iambic
   and Moravian Music Foundation
TUNE: Popular melody, Hans Leo Hassler (1601);       PASSION CHORALE (151 A)
   C. Gregor *Choralbuch* (1784)

# Jesus, Lord of Life and Light

**26**

Capo 3:

1. Je - sus, Lord of Life and Light, ev - 'ry soul's sal - va - tion,
2. Will - ing - ly you bore the cross, shared our pain dis - tress - ing,
3. Pen - te - cost and tongues of flame gave your church true pow - er

glow - ing hope in sin's dark night, love's bright af - firm - a - tion:
died to mend our trag - ic loss, turn - ing curse to bless - ing.
to pro - claim your sav - ing name in each place and hour.

on the earth on Christ - mas night you were born in meek - ness,
Eas - ter morn - ing saw you rise, hope and joy re - stor - ing,
Je - sus, Lord of Life and Light, all earth's lights tran - scend - ing:

leav - ing all your heav'n - ly might to em - brace our weak - ness.
as dis - ci - ples' won - d'ring eyes glowed with love, a - dor - ing.
help us by your Spir - it's might live your love un - end - ing.

TEXT: C. Daniel Crews (2001). © 2013 by Interprovincial Board of Communication and Moravian Music Foundation

TUNE: Jan Roh (1544), alt.

7.6.7.6.D. Trochaic

GAUDEAMUS PARITER

# 27 Transfigured on the Mountain High

1. Trans-fig-ured on the moun-tain high, with friends all trem-bling
2. As did those friends so long a-go, we of-ten fail to

at the sight and an-cient proph-ets stand-ing nigh, Christ's
com-pre-hend that from Christ's wounds such love did flow and

glo-ry shone in ra-diant light. "This is my Son; you
on this love we can de-pend. Christ's sac-ri-fice, a

need not fear. He comes to give you life a-new. Pay
gift so dear, re-mains our hope, our shel-ter true. To-

TEXT: Gilbert L. Frank (2000). © 2000 by Gilbert L. Frank
TUNE: Herrnhut (c. 1735); C. Gregor *Choralbuch* (1784)

L.M.D.
PILGRIMAGE (166 A)

heed to him while he is here, for on the cross he'll die for you."
day, dear Lord, dis - pel our fear as in our faith we wel-come you.

# O Christ, We Celebrate Your Birth   28

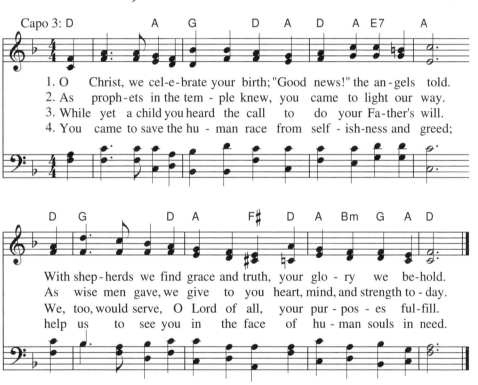

1. O Christ, we cel-e-brate your birth; "Good news!" the an-gels told.
2. As proph-ets in the tem - ple knew, you came to light our way.
3. While yet a child you heard the call to do your Fa-ther's will.
4. You came to save the hu - man race from self - ish-ness and greed;

With shep-herds we find grace and truth, your glo - ry we be-hold.
As wise men gave, we give to you heart, mind, and strength to - day.
We, too, would serve, O Lord of all, your pur - pos - es ful-fill.
help us to see you in the face of hu - man souls in need.

5. You offered hope to those oppressed;
   to captives, brought release.
   You lived your life in righteousness,
   for justice, love, and peace.

6. Lord, let the Scriptures speak to us,
   your Spirit guide our ways,
   that we may live to do your works
   and to declare your praise.

TEXT: Carl Helmich, Jr. © 2013 by Interprovincial Board of Communication
and Moravian Music Foundation.
TUNE: Este's *Psalter* (1592)

C.M.

WINCHESTER, OLD (14 Z)

# 29 Christ Is Born!

1. Christ is born! Christ is born! Proph-ets' word of old fore-told the com-ing of a Sav-ior who would re-main for-ev-er God's gift of love, a
2. An-gels sing! An-gels sing: Glo-ry be to God on high! For un-to us a Sav-ior is born in hum-ble man-ger. Go seek him now, a-
3. Shep-herds come! Shep-herds come quick-ly to the man-ger bed in rev-'rent awe and won-der to see the in-fant Je-sus, on bend-ed knee, a-
4. We re-joice! We re-joice! Christ, the cen-ter of our faith, in God's great love and mer-cy, con-fers grace nev-er ceas-ing. To love our God, Christ

TEXT: Gilbert H. Frank (1983, rev. 2002). © 2002 by Gilbert H. Frank
TUNE: Georg Joseph (1657), alt. C. Gregor *Choralbuch* (1784)

3.3.7.7.7.7.7.4.4.4.4.7. Mixed
CHURCH, REJOICE! (225 A)

Prom - ise, the Prince of Peace, Mes - si - ah.
dore him, in Da - vid's cit - y, ho - ly.
dor - ing, for such a gift, re - joic - ing!
calls us; to love all souls, Christ leads us!

Long ex - pec - ted! In - car - na - tion! Won-drous Je - sus!
Al - le - lu - ia! An - gels' sto - ry: to all peo - ple,
God is with us! Shout with glo - ry! God is with us!
Earth-ly mis - sion! Cru - ci - fix - ion! Re - sur - rec - tion!

Our sal - va - tion! God the Son to earth is come.
peace and joy!___ God the Son to earth is come.
Spread the sto - ry! God the Son to earth is come.
Af - fir - ma - tion! God the Son is with us still.

# 30       Lord, Son of God

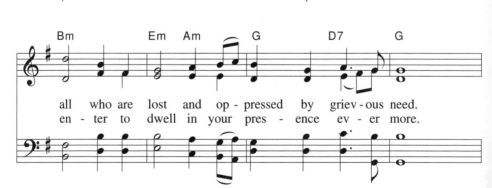

1. Lord, Son of God, our Pas-chal Lamb vic-to-rious, we
2. Lord, Son of God, our Pas-chal Lamb vic-to-rious, we

1. fol-low your ban-ner wher-ev-er you may lead; we
2. fol-low your ban-ner to heav-en's o-pen door, where

1. go forth to bear good news of your sal-va-tion to
2. all who have found the joy of your sal-va-tion may

1. all who are lost and op-pressed by griev-ous need.
2. en-ter to dwell in your pres-ence ev-er more.

TEXT: Dirk French (2003)
TUNE: Dirk French (2003)
© 2003 by Dirk French.

11.12.12.12.13.12.12.12
LORD, SON OF GOD

THE SAVING WORK OF CHRIST

# 31 Shepherds Watch as Night Is Falling

1. Shep-herds watch as night is fall-ing when good news the
2. Wise men from the East will fol-low in the sky a
3. Joined to-geth-er here we gath-er to pro-claim this

an-gels bring; "Glo-ry to the Lord most ho-ly, now is
shin-ing star, lead-ing to a child most roy-al for whom
ho-ly birth; come, Lord Je-sus, with com-pas-sion, fill us

born a Child, a King!" Through the night their songs re-sound-ing,
three will trav-el far; gifts they bear, most pre-cious, cost-ly,
with a-bun-dant worth. Hu-man moth-er, Ho-ly Fa-ther,

glo-ry lights the sky a-bove; shep-herds hur-ry to see the
fit-ting hom-age to the King; miles they trav-el to of-fer
born to save from sin and fear; with great joy we raise our

TEXT: Ruth Cole Burcaw (2010). © 2013 by Interprovincial Board of
Communication and Moravian Music Foundation
TUNE: Rowland Hugh Prichard (1885)

8.7.8.7.D.

HYFRYDOL

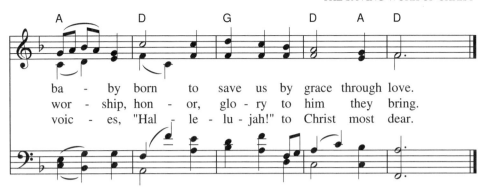

ba - by born to save us by grace through love.
wor - ship, hon - or, glo - ry to him they bring.
voic - es, "Hal - le - lu - jah!" to Christ most dear.

## Jesus, Once in Galilee 32

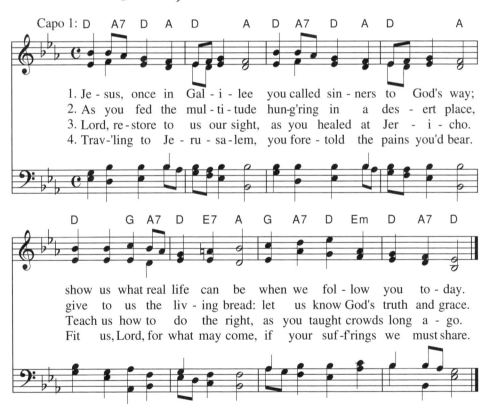

1. Je - sus, once in Gal - i - lee you called sin - ners to God's way;
2. As you fed the mul - ti - tude hun-g'ring in a des - ert place,
3. Lord, re - store to us our sight, as you healed at Jer - i - cho.
4. Trav-'ling to Je - ru - sa-lem, you fore - told the pains you'd bear.

show us what real life can be when we fol - low you to - day.
give to us the liv - ing bread: let us know God's truth and grace.
Teach us how to do the right, as you taught crowds long a - go.
Fit us, Lord, for what may come, if your suf-f'rings we must share.

5. Help us yield our will to God
   with you in Gethsemane,
   by our deeds proclaim your word
   and your death at Calvary.

6. Risen Christ, redeem our life,
   as we take up our own cross,
   work and pray and sacrifice
   to advance your kingdom's cause.

TEXT: Carl Helmich, Jr. (2011) © 2013 by Interprovincial Board of     7.7.7.7. Trochaic
    Communication and Moravian Music Foundation
TUNE: Herrnhut (c. 1735); C. Gregor *Choralbuch* (1784)     HERRNHUT (11 A)

# 33 Morning Star, O Cheering Sight

1. Morn-ing Star, O cheer-ing sight! Come and light this dark earth's night. Morn-ing Star, O cheer-ing sight! Come and light this dark earth's night! Je-sus mine, in me shine, in me shine, Je-sus mine, fill my heart with light di - vine.

2. Morn-ing Star, your glo-ry bright far ex-cels the sun's clear light. Morn-ing Star, your glo-ry bright far ex-cels the sun's clear light. Je-sus be, con-stant-ly, con-stant-ly, Je-sus be more than thou-sand suns to me.

3. Your pure light, O Morn-ing Star, of-fers hope both near and far. Your pure light, O Morn-ing Star, of-fers hope both near and far. Now you're known, Christ a-lone, Christ a-lone, now you're known! Our great Sav-ior, God's dear Son!

4. Morn-ing Star, my soul's true light, hur-ry now, make bright my night! Morn-ing Star, my soul's true light, hur-ry now, make bright my night! Je-sus mine, in me shine, in me shine, Je-sus mine, fill my heart with light di - vine.

TEXT: Johann Scheffler (1657). Tr. Bennet Harvey, Jr. (1885), alt. Karen Banks and Carol J. Vogler (2011). © 2013 Interprovincial Board of Communication and Moravian Music Foundation.

TUNE: Francis Florentine Hagen (1836)

7.7.3.3.7.

HAGEN (310 B)

# We Have Come From Foreign Lands 34

1. We have come from foreign lands, bearing gifts across the sands.
2. "Go to Bethlehem," as told in the Hebrew prophet's word.
3. Kneel we now, adore the one, Lord of all, yet mother's son;

We have journeyed from the east many days with slave and beast;
"Travel on, the place is near; bring back news I long to hear."
offer myrrh, gold, frankincense, and our hearts with righteousness.

traveling by night, a star now we follow from afar,
So that star shone bright to show that small house where we must go,
Holy mother, holy Child, as we bow our hearts are blessed

to Jerusalem to meet with King Herod, there to speak.
there the child was to be found, there we lay our gifts around.
with the promise giv'n to all: Prince of Peace, now God with us!

TEXT: Jill B. Bruckart (2011)
TUNE: Jill B. Bruckart (2011)
Text and tune © 2011 by Jill B. Bruckart

7.7.7.7.D.
EPIPHANY

**35** # Sweet Baby Jesus

Sweet _____ ba - by Je - sus, _____

I _____ love _____ you, Lord. _____

TEXT: Steve Gray (1990)
TUNE: Steve Gray (1990)
© 1990 by Steve Gray

Irregular
SWEET BABY JESUS

Hum - ble child, ___ yet born a ___ King,

I ___ praise and a-dore. _____

I can see heav - en-ly an - gels ___ sing-ing round your bed.
You are the Son ___ of God, ___ the ___ Sav-ior of hu-man-kind,

The shep-herds are kneel - ing in awe.
you are the light_____ of the world.

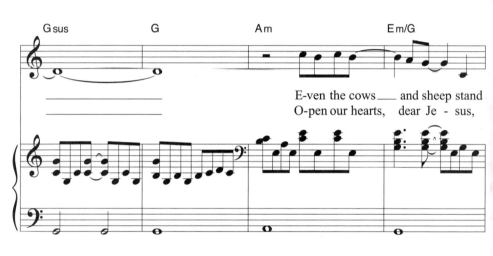

E-ven the cows__ and sheep stand
O-pen our hearts, dear Je - sus,

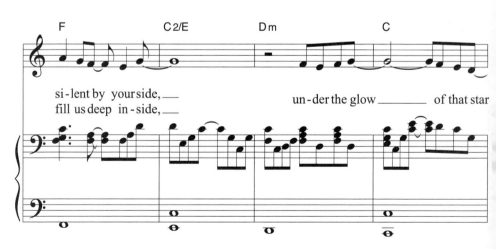

si-lent by your side,__
fill us deep in-side,__

un-der the glow_____ of that star

# 36 In This Crowd Sing Out Loud

In this crowd sing out loud: Glo - ry to the One!

God has made things per - son - al by send-ing us the Son!

In this crowd sing out loud: Glo - ry! Al - le - lu!

Cel - e - brate the birth of Christ, the day of his de - but.

TEXT: Christine Sobania Johnson (2004). © 2004 by Christine Sobania Johnson
TUNE: James Lord Pierpont (1850)

6.6.6.6.D.
JINGLE BELLS

1. The faith-ful wait-ed long for God to in-ter-vene, to
2. God's love is for us all; so let there be no doubt. The

rule with pow'r and might, to give them what they dreamed. _____
poor, the weak, the small: _____ no one is left out! The

What a big sur-prise! The Sav-ior was a child! The
rea-son Je-sus came: God want-ed to be near; God

Christ-mas sto-ry goes to show God's plans are real-ly wild!
want-ed to draw close to us, and that is why we cheer!

# 37    The Manger in My Heart

Moderato (♩ = ca. 60)

1. In the qui - et of the
2. Be - fore me stands a
3. In teen - age years when
4. With chil - dren gone she
5. The Christ Child is not

morn - ing there is Christ - mas in the air. I
lit - tle child with dirt - caked hands and face. ——
Christ - mas myths of rein - deer have all gone, we
lived a - lone, her age was well ad - vanced, and
far a - way. The man - ger's here to see, for

search the sky for yon - der star but can - not find it
Hun - ger, fear, and sor - row put each tear - drop in its
strug - gle in our dai - ly lives to know what's right and
e - ven though her bones were slow, her eyes would skip and
sa - ges and for shep - herds too; he's born for you and

TEXT: Rick Beck (1987)
TUNE: Rick Beck (1987)
© 2013 by Interprovincial Board of Communication
and Moravian Music Foundation

MANGER

there.    I long to know the Ho - ly Child. His
place.    Could hope from God be real to him to
wrong.    ___ If you seek to find the place where
dance.    I saw her on the street one day with
me.    If Christ - mas is to live for you, then

sto - ry's in the Book, but it hap - pened once so
set his spir - it free? And with his eyes he
Christ - mas bells had rung, go deep with - in your
young and old a - like, in - vit - ing all to
look and see the star a - bove the heads of

long a - go I don't know where to look. _____
touched my soul, and this he said to me: _____
soul now with these words up - on your tongue. _____
cel - e - brate the Sav - ior born that night. _____
those a - round, of neigh - bors near and far. _____

Christ - mas lives with - in my heart. The

THE SAVING WORK OF CHRIST

sto-ry  is a - live to-day, I  know that I'm a part.     If    you

seek      the  man - ger    too,     to - geth-er  let us

jour-ney  on to  where God's love is  true.      true.   To-

geth-er  let us jour-ney on to where God's  love      is true.

# Light of the World

1. Light of the world, come near and bless your chil-dren here be - low, who in your house your name con - fess; on us your grace be - stow.
2. Light of the world, you are the way; to you our - selves we give, to share your death on this dark day, and by your light to live.
3. Light of the world, you light our way, cast - ing out doubts and tears, chang-ing our dark - ness in - to day, heal - ing our hurts and fears.
4. Light of the world, you touched the ill, the out-cast and the poor, show - ing your love to - day, and still more bless-ings yet in store.

5. Light of the world, you prayed, forgive; forgiveness daily gave.
   Forgive us now the lives we live; we look to you to save.

6. Light of the world, your work is through; our vigil now we keep.
   In this dark hour we pray for you; and pray for all who sleep.

7. Light of the world, your torment done, at rest within the grave;
   waiting the glorious Easter dawn, for you and those you save.

TEXT: St. 1, Charles E. W. Harvey (1846-1922); st. 2-7, Richard L. Bruckart (2011).
St. 2-7 © 2011 by Richard L. Bruckart
TUNE: John B. Dykes (1866)

C.M.

ST. AGNES (14 Cc)

# 39    A Kind Word Praises God

Moderato (♩= ca. 84-92)

1. — God is with us in ev-'ry-thing we do, tak-ing
2. — Love is kind and re-joic-es in the right: it is
3. God loves the per-son who——— loves to give, giv-ing
4. — Our re-ward for the kind-ness that we show comes from

note of ev-'ry thought-ful——— deed;———"As you have
right to share our gifts from God a-bove,——— So
cheer-ful-ly her smile, his time, their wealth.——— You may
see-ing that God's plan will be ful-filled;——— our joy

done un-to one—— of the least—— of these,—— you have
love,—— faith, hope a-bide, these three which we should share, but the
ask what you have—— that is worth of-fer-ing,——— you can
comes from prais-ing God with all our—— strength,——— so

TEXT: R. L. Rominger (1973)
TUNE: R. L. Rominger (1973)
Text and music © 1978 by R. L. Rominger, III

Irregular
A KIND WORD

al - so done___ un - to me."___
great - est of___ these is love.___
grac - ious - ly___ give your - self.___
praise the Lord then, do God's will.___

A

kind word prais-es God. A kind word prais-es

God.___ A gen-tle hand___ can___ bless the soul.___ A

kind word prais-es___ God.___

**40** **Sing for Joy!**

1. Sing for joy! Sing pas-sion-ate-ly strong. Sing as though your great-est gift of love could be your song. Sing for peace. Sing qui-et-ly, but clear._____ Sing a gen-tle phrase as though you're whis-p'ring in God's ear. Mu-sic is a

2. Sing for help when trou-bles o-ver-whelm. Cry out your la-ments when dark-ness spreads a-cross your realm. Sing for thanks when bless-ings o-ver-flow._____ Sing a-bout con-tent-ed-ness that you have come to know. Mu-sic is a

3. Sing, just sing, as you were meant to do! Vo-cal-ize and har-mo-nize and hum the whole day through. Sing toward heav-en, sing a-loud on earth._____ Wor-ship God with hymns of praise! Sing now for all you're worth! Mu-sic is a

TEXT: Christine Sobania Johnson (2011). © 2011 by Christine Sobania Johnson
TUNE: Francis Florentine Hagen (1836)

9.13.9.13.5.5.8.
HAGEN (310 B)

prayer. Sing it ev-'ry - where. God is ev-'ry - where, lis-t'ning to a
prayer. Sing it ev-'ry - where. God is ev-'ry - where, an - swer-ing a
prayer. Sing it ev-'ry - where. God is ev-'ry - where. "A-men!" to that

prayer. Come to God through a mel - o - dy.
prayer. Some-times God's voice___ comes as song.
prayer. Bless God and be___ blessed in song.

# Sometimes, When I Pray    41

Sometimes, when I pray,
I bow my head, cup my hands,
And hold them out in front of me as though I were:

*Raising Living Water to my lips*

*Waiting to receive the Bread of Life*

*Offering up my heart, my soul, my strength*

*Sheltering a small spark of the Light of the World*

*Setting free a cloud-white dove to find us a token of Peace*

Sometimes, when I pray.

Brian Dixon © by Brian Dixon

# 42 There Is No Fear in Love

TEXT: 1 John 4:18
TUNE: David Melby-Gibbons. © 2013 by Interprovincial Board of Communication
and Moravian Music Foundation

Irregular
NO FEAR

# 43     **Sing Praise to God**

1. Sing praise to God the Fa - ther, sing praise to God a - bove, for all God has cre - a - ted, for dai - ly gifts of love.
2. Sing praise to Christ the Sav - ior, sing praise to Christ our Lord, who came on earth a - mong us, and showed us God's true word.
3. Sing praise to God the Spir - it, our Com - fort-er and Friend, whose teach - ing us of Je - sus shall nev - er have an end.
4. Sing praise to God the Fa - ther, sing praise to God the Son, sing praise to God the Spir - it, e - ter - nal Three in One.

TEXT: Albert H. Frank (1999). © 2012 by Erdmute Frank
TUNE: Nola Reed Knouse (2000). © 2013 by Interprovincial Board of Communication
and Moravian Music Foundation

7.6.7.6
SING PRAISE

# Just As I Am

1. Just as I am, with-out one plea but that your blood was shed for me, and that you call me, e - ven me, O Lamb of God, I come, I come.

2. Just as I am, weak flesh and mind; some-times my soul to you is blind, but now, this day, I search, I find. O Je - sus, Friend, I come, I come.

3. Just as I am, my wants de - layed; I've claimed your Word, I've worked, I've prayed. As life un - folds my faith dis - played, O Je - sus, Lord, I come, I come.

4. Just as I am, trans - formed by love to know the truth that dwells a - bove. De - scend to me, O heav'n - ly dove. O Spir - it Ho - ly, I come, I come.

5. Just as I am, this joy - ful day, I choose to - day to walk the Way. O let me al - ways near you stay, O God of all, I come, I come.

TEXT: St 1. Charlotte Elliott (1836), alt; st. 2-5, Willard R. Harstine (2009).
© 2013 by Interprovincial Board of Communication
and Moravian Music Foundation
TUNE: William B. Bradbury (1849)

8.8.8.6.

WOODWORTH (277 E)

# 45 Walk With Me Each Day, Savior

1. Walk with me each day, Savior; I'm apt to lose my way.
2. Walk with me each day, Jesus, for rocky is the path.
3. Walk with me each day, Savior, and be my only guide.
4. Walk with me each day, Jesus, and let my heart be true.

When with each step I falter, then let me hear you say,
Grant faith and reassurance that you will hold me fast.
My heart is often hardened, my soul is full of pride.
I'll strive to show to others that caring comes from you.

"My love is always waiting, I stand beside the door.
Oh, make your love a beacon, a guiding ray of light.
Oh, help me find the way, Lord, your child to truly be.
May all whom I encounter see your love in my face,

If you will only open, I'll love you evermore."
that I may ever follow and not be lost in night.
I know your love is faithful, complete, and full, and free.
and may I be a vessel of your enduring grace.

TEXT: Susan Cox Starbuck (2000). © 2013 by Susan Cox Starbuck
TUNE: Popular melody, Hans Leo Hassler (1601); C. Gregor *Choralbuch* (1784)  PASSION CHORALE (151 A)

7.6.7.6.D.

# Journey

Moderato (♩ = 72)

1. Like A - bra - ham and Sa - rah too, I jour-ney with my Lord. There's al - ways some - thing I can do, I jour-ney with my Lord. And if I lis - ten when I'm told by God who calls me to

2. *(Insert verses 2a - 2d as desired)*

3. We are dis - ci - ples of our day, we jour-ney with our Lord. Let's help each oth - er on the Way, we jour-ney with our Lord. And with his love he took our shame, he e - ven dared to take

TEXT: Rick Beck (2010)
TUNE: Rick Beck (2010)
© 2013 by Interprovincial Board of Communication
and Moravian Music Foundation

Irregular
JOURNEY

FAITH

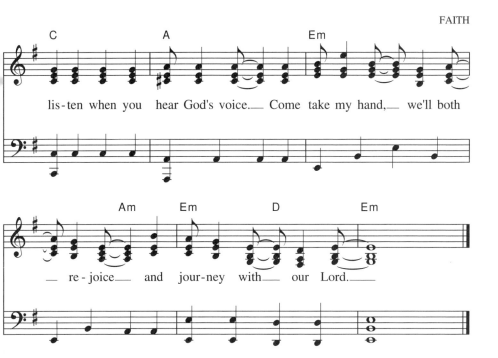

lis-ten when you hear God's voice.— Come take my hand,— we'll both

re - joice— and jour-ney with— our Lord.—

2a.  Like Moses and his wand'ring band, I journey with my Lord.
     Who trusted God out in the sand, I journey with my Lord.
     And what I need God will supply; abundant grace I can't deny.
     The great I AM is my ally, I journey with my Lord.

2b.  Like Esther with her grace and charm, I journey with my Lord.
     So others will not come to harm, I journey with my Lord.
     To please the king became his wife, and then spoke up to save a life.
     I too can ease another's strife. I journey with my Lord.

2c.  Like Solomon who was so wise, I journey with my Lord.
     Built God a home, a heav'nly prize. I journey with my Lord.
     My heart's the temple of God's will where I will worship God until
     the holy promise is fulfilled. I journey with my Lord.

2d.  Like Paul who crashed his faithful boat, I journey with my Lord.
     Sometimes I find it hard to float. I journey with my Lord.
     Before I have a chance to blink, my burdens take me to the brink -
     cast off my sins before I sink. I journey with my Lord.

# 47 Bliss Beyond Compare

1. Bliss be-yond com-pare,_____
2. When the Lord ap - pears,_____
3. Then all grief is drowned;_____
4. Je - sus is my joy,_____

which in Christ I share!_____ He's my on - ly joy
this my spir - it cheers;___ when, his love to me
pure de - light is found,___ joy and peace in his
there-fore blessed am I;_____ O, his mer-cy is

TEXT: Gottfried Arnold (1666-1714). Mor. tr. (1754).
      Recast Frederick William Foster (1789)
TUNE: Samuel J. Gray (2011). © 2011 by Samuel J. Gray

5.5.8.8.5.

BLISS (68 E

D/A      Em

_ and treas - ure;    taste - less is all world-
_ re - veal - ing,    he, the Sun of grace,
_ sal - va - tion,    heav'n - ly bliss and con -
_ un - bound - ed, _    all my hope on him_

F♯      Bm

- ly pleas - ure, when _ in Christ I share_
_ with heal - ing in_ his beams ap - pears,_
- so - la - tion. Ev - 'ry grief is drowned
_ is ground - ed; Je - sus is_ my joy,_

Em7      A7sus      A7      D

_ bliss be - yond com-pare._
_ this my spir - it cheers._
_ where such bliss is found._
_ there - fore blessed am I._

# 48 Lord, Have Mercy

**Moderato** (♩ = 90)

1. Lord, have mer - cy up - on my soul; the war with -
2. Fa - ther, turn me to-ward your view, to seek your
3. Sav - ior, guard me from false pride; your grace is
4. Spir - it, fill me with your strength; my own re -
5. Christ, re - new me with your peace; my spir - it

TEXT and MUSIC: R. L. Rominger, III (1988)

7.9.13.7.

C

in     seems out  of con-trol._____     Take  this
will    in    all that I   do._____     Though  I
all     I    need to  a - bide._____     Take  my
solve  will  fail me  at  length._____     Set   my
yearns  to   see you in -crease._____     Take  this

Am          G          F          G          Dm          G

bit - ter - ness     and     turn     it  in - to     grate - ful - ness.
feel  wrongs  done,  please,   teach  me  to    for - give  each  one.
van - i - ty       and     clothe me  in     hu - mil - i - ty.____
spir - it    free      to     wait  up-on  you    pa - tient-ly.____
rest - less - ness   and     calm  me by  your    gra - cious-ness.

C              G              C              *Last time*

Lord,  have  mer - cy up - on   my  soul.
Fa - ther,  turn  me to-ward your  view.
Sav - ior,  guard me   from false pride.
Spir - it    fill   me   with your strength.
Lord,  have  mer - cy up - on   my  soul.

# 49 Come, Follow Me

TEXT: Rick Beck (2012); see Matthew 2, Mark 10, Matthew 14, Luke 10
TUNE: Rick Beck (2012)
© by Interprovincial Board of Communication
and Moravian Music Foundation

7.7.7.7.7.7.9. with Refrain
COME FOLLOW ME

Je-sus Christ said, Hey! Come, fol-low me!___

1. Three wise men did see a star___ shin - ing in the
2. Bar - ti - mae - us was so blind___ he was of - ten
3. Je - sus called from on the sea,___ "Pe - ter, won't you
4. Mar - tha said, "It is - n't fair.___ Mar - y is just

east so far.___ Prom - ise is what they did find,___
left be - hind.___ E - ven though his hopes were dim___
come to me?"___ Would he trust his faith - ful guide___
sit - ting there.___ I've got all this work to do.___

far be - yond the hu - man kind.___ Now we lis - ten
he knew Christ could cure___ him.___ In the dark - ness
on the sea by Je - sus' side?___ Now he calls us
She spends all her time with you."___ In our work and

for his voice;— trust-ing God, we make a choice.
of our night— Je - sus is our guid - ing light.
to be brave, liv - ing life as one who's saved.
in our play,— all the things we do to - day,—

Start your jour-ney now right where you are.—
He's the hope for all of hu - man - kind.—
Je - sus calls us out to set us free.—
give it all to Christ as liv - ing prayer.—

*After v. 1-3, repeat from beginning*
*After v. 4, continue*

The Lord said: Come! Come, fol-low me.—

Drop your nets be - side the sea.— He said, come! Come,

**50**

# By Galilee

1. By Ga-li - lee_____ I met the
2. By Ga-li - lee_____ I heard him
3. By Ga-li - lee_____ I made a

Sav - ior;_____ by Ga-li - lee_____ I heard him call;_____ by Ga-li-
whis - per;_____ by Ga-li - lee_____ he touched my heart;_____ by Ga-li-
prom - ise;_____ by Ga-li - lee_____ I made a vow;_____ by Ga-li-

TEXT: Lahoma Gray (1985)
TUNE: Lahoma Gray; arr. Steve Gray and Sam Gray. © by Steve Gray and Sam Gray

9.8.9.9. with Refrain
BY GALILEE

lee____ I felt his pre-sence, and I'll nev-er be the same a - gain.____
lee____ he stood be - side me, and I'll nev-er be the same a - gain.____
lee____ he drew me to him, and I'll nev-er be the same a - gain.____

*Refrain*

By Ga-li - lee____ I saw the splen-dor____ of all the love____ he has to

give.____ It filled my cup____ to o-ver-flow-ing,____ and I'll

nev-er be the same a - gain.____ gain, and I'll nev-er be the same a-gain.

# 51 I Will Trust in God

1. I will trust in God, my strength and shield; my
soul will re-joice; I will be healed. My heart will re-nounce the
sin of pride: se-rene-ly in peace I will a-bide.

2. I will seek God's help in all my life; to
fol-low the Way in calm or strife; to flour-ish in faith with
God as guide: en-fold-ed in love I will a-bide.

TEXT: Paul Schick (2012), adapted from Psalm 131, Psalm 25
TUNE: Paul Schick (2012)
© 2012 by Paul Schick

9.9.9.9.

TRUST AND ABIDE

# In Our Churches, In Our Churches 52

Capo 3: D      A   D      G   D      G   A

1. In our church-es, in our church-es, o - pen wide the door;
2. No dis - tinc-tions, no dis - tinc-tions shall di - vide us here;
3. Show God's mer - cy, show God's mer - cy un - to one and all;

love should al - ways, love should al - ways jour-ney with the poor.
God's im - par - tial, God's im - par - tial: ev - 'ry - one is dear;
with - out judg-ing, with - out judg-ing as we heed our call;

So - cial sta - tus has no say in the pat-tern of our way.
let this be our church's goal: to in - clude each need - y soul;
this is how our church shall be: filled with love and lib - er - ty,

All are wel-come, all are wel-come, rich - es we ig - nore.
grace is giv - en, grace is giv - en: Christ has made that clear.
in the Spir - it, in the Spir - it of our Sav - ior's law.

TEXT: William E. Gramley (1993). © 2013 by Interprovincial Board of Communication
    and Moravian Music Foundation
TUNE: Melody, Johann Georg Hille (1739); J. D. Grimm *Choralbuch* (1755);
    C. Gregor *Choralbuch* (1784), alt.

8.5.8.5.7.7.8.5.

SERVICE (56 A)

# 53 Ev'ry God-Given Day

1. Ev-'ry God-giv-en day of-fers chanc-es to grow, to
2. Ev-'ry God-giv-en day of-fers chanc-es to care for
3. Ev-'ry God-giv-en day of-fers chanc-es a-new to

chal-lenge our faith and to strength-en it so, to
loved ones and strang-ers, to nur-ture and share in their
show God's com-pas-sion, as Christ bids us to, for

in-crease our knowl-edge, and there-fore we pray to
joys and con-cerns; thus we grate-ful-ly pray to
all God's cre-a-tion, so hum-bly we pray to

God in thanks-giv-ing for ev-'ry new day.
God in thanks-giv-ing for ev-'ry new day.
God in thanks-giv-ing for ev-'ry new day.

TEXT: Barbara Prillaman (2009). © 2009 by Barbara Prillaman
TUNE: Hubert W. Fort (2009). © 2013 by Interprovincial Board of Communication
    and Moravian Music Foundation

6.6.5.6.6.5.6.5.
LILLIAN

# Jesus, Your Arms Are Open 54

Capo 1: D

1. Je - sus, your arms are o - pen to chil - dren full of life,
2. Je - sus, your arms are o - pen to chil - dren filled with fear,
3. Je - sus, your arms are o - pen to chil - dren filled with grace,

who know a play - ful child-hood with laugh - ter free of strife,
who want for love and nur - ture. To your side draw them near.
who trust you with - out ques - tion, who know your warm em - brace.

a pre - view of the king-dom per - fect - ed by your love,
From tow'r - ing threats de - liv - er, pre - serve them from all harm,
We look to their ex - am - ple, their sim - ple faith, so true;

sur - round - ed by the pres - ence of peace come from a - bove.
stretch out our hands with your love; their qui - et fears dis - arm.
Je - sus, your arms are o - pen for us to live in you.

TEXT: John D. Rights (2000). © 2000 by Mary White Rights
TUNE: Samuel Sebastian Wesley (1864)

7.6.7.6.D.
AURELIA (151 L)

LOVE

# 55 Sing We Now With Joyfulness

*Refrain*

*Unison*

Sing we now with joy - ful - ness, our voic-es joined as one.

Christ is our true hap - pi - ness; all praise to God's dear Son.

*Fine*

1. We lift our voic-es sing - ing in grate - ful thanks and praise
2. In fel - low-ship to - geth - er, all wel - come as his friends,
3. Christ calls us to be part-ners, to fol - low him in love,

to Christ whose love sur - rounds us through-out our life-long days.
u - nit - ed by his fa - vor, and love that nev-er ends:
to serve as his dis - ci - ples, and live with him a - bove.

*D.C.*

TEXT: Thom Stapleton (2004) © 2004 by Thom Stapleton
TUNE: Trad. English melody. Harm. Nola Reed Knouse

7.6.7.6. with Refrain
ROYAL OAK

# Let Justice Roll On

1. Let jus - tice roll on like the riv - ers of time, and
2. We must not be ar - ro - gant, boast - ful, un - kind, but
3. Our gifts, though di - verse, form a cov - e - nant bond, which
4. In things non - es - sen - tial each one may be free; in

right - eous - ness flow in con - tin - u - ous stream, that
prac - tice com - pas - sion and be of one mind. May
binds us to - geth - er that we may re - spond in
God's law of love, though, we all must a - gree. May

we in God's wis - dom and love may a - bide and
we not be proud of our call - ing or place, but
strength and re - la - tion - ship, one fam - i - ly, in
each per - son fol - low our Sav - ior's com - mand and

live in com - mu - ni - ty, not self - ish pride.
treat all as mem - bers of one com - mon race.
ac - tion and at - ti - tude live self - less - ly.
love one an - oth - er with warm heart and hand.

TEXT: E. Artis W. Weber (2002). © 2013 by Interprovincial Board of Communication    11.11.11.11. Anapestic
    and Moravian Music Foundation
TUNE: Herrnhut (c. 1740); C. Gregor *Choralbuch* (1784)                          CONFESSION (39 A)

# 57 Love Will Find You

Love will find you if you'll o-pen up your heart and let it in, let it in; love will find you. Won't you o-pen up your life so love comes in, love comes in? in? It'll come in. 1.God is wait-ing 2.God is call-ing

*To verses*

*3rd time*

*Verses*

*Fine*

TEXT and MUSIC: Brad Bennett (1983). © 1983 by Brad Bennett

Irregular
LOVE WILL FIND YOU

for us all— to wake up from our sleep. If we'd on-ly
out for us— if we'd on-ly hear. Why not be ad-

hear the call— such love we would re-ceive.— Love will
ven-tur-ous— and let the love come near.—

## We Want to Love 58

1. We want to love our God on high with heart and soul and might;
2. Our love of self is ba-sic, too, and not a sign of pride;
3. This love of God and self and all re-flects di-vin-i-ty.
4. O give us grace, dear God a-bove, to live in har-mo-ny

we can-not pass our neigh-bor by, for love keeps both in sight.
O may this be our world-wide view: to love from deep in-side.
It is the es-sence of God's law to guide hu-man-i-ty.
and show the splen-dor of your love as chil-dren grate-ful-ly.

TEXT: William E. Gramley (1993). © 2013 by Interprovincial Board of Communication
and Moravian Music Foundation
TUNE: Johann Georg Christian Störl (1710); C. Gregor *Choralbuch* (1784), alt.

C.M.

HAB DANK, O JESU

# 59     Friends, Welcome One Another

1. Friends, wel-come one an-oth-er as Christ has wel-comed you.
2. Our mod-el is the Sav-ior whose grace is la-beled "free."

Say "yes" to sis-ter, broth-er, and that way live a-new.
We of-fer to the neigh-bor Christ's hos-pi-tal-i-ty.

Our life to-geth-er is a sign of life to come in God's de-sign.
In this way God is glo-ri-fied, not by the vic-t'ry of "our side."

The strong and weak will live as one, thanks to the ris-en Son.
We wel-come just as Christ, and then we praise the Lord! A-men.

TEXT: Michael Kinnamon (2002). © 2013 by Interprovincial Board of Communication
    and Moravian Music Foundation
TUNE: Johann Christian Bechler (1784-1857)

7.6.7.6.8.8.8.6.

BECHLER (159 D)

# The Lord Will Come

1. The Lord will come, as well we know, just
2. Sur - prise will come so sud - den - ly, like
3. Build up each oth - er in the faith, push

as a thief at night. Sleep not nor won - der
pangs of giv - ing birth; but chil - dren of the
e - vil thoughts a - side; en - cour - age oth - ers,

what to do as___ chil - dren of the light.
light and day keep___ vig - il, stay a - lert.
as you do, thus___ we in Christ a - bide.

TEXT: Barbara Jo Strauss (1996), based on 1 Thessalonians 5:1-11.
© 1996 by Barbara Jo Strauss
TUNE: Carl C. Gläser (1828). Arr. Lowell Mason (1839)

C.M.

AZMON

# 61 We're Heaven Bound

Moderato (♩= 84-90)

We're heav-en bound,

that's the place we want to be;——we're heav-en bound,

it was made for you and me.——We're heav-en bound,

TEXT and MUSIC: Rick Beck
© 2013 by Interprovincial Board of Communication
and Moravian Music Foundation

8.6.8.6.8.6.4.6. with refrain
HEAVEN BOUND

where Cre - a - tor fills the soul,___ where

peace and joy and love are in con-trol.___

*Fine* *Verses*

(3.)The

*Fine*

*Verses* G                                                      D

1. When we're poor in    spir - it, when___ we  jour - ney   on    the Way,
2. Meek - ness    is    a    bless-ing  though we're told    it    has   no worth.
3. mer - cy    that   I    of - fer you___ will  come right back   to    me.

# 62 I'm Making All Things New

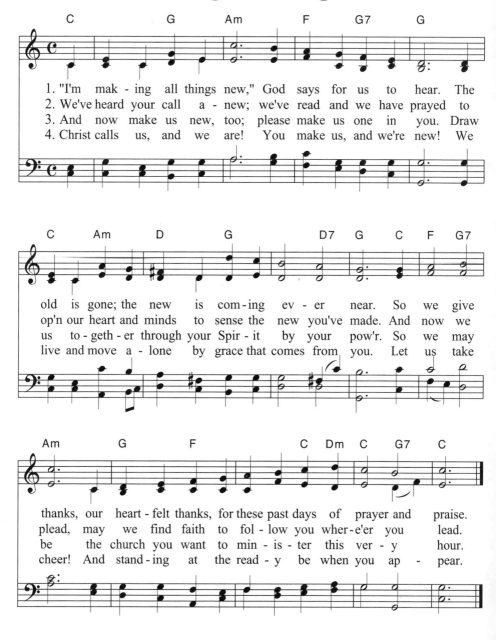

1. "I'm mak-ing all things new," God says for us to hear. The
2. We've heard your call a - new; we've read and we have prayed to
3. And now make us new, too; please make us one in you. Draw
4. Christ calls us, and we are! You make us, and we're new! We

old is gone; the new is com-ing ev - er near. So we give
op'n our heart and minds to sense the new you've made. And now we
us to - geth - er through your Spir - it by your pow'r. So we may
live and move a - lone by grace that comes from you. Let us take

thanks, our heart-felt thanks, for these past days of prayer and praise.
plead, may we find faith to fol - low you wher-e'er you lead.
be the church you want to min - is - ter this ver - y hour.
cheer! And stand-ing at the read - y be when you ap - pear.

TEXT: C. Riddick Weber (2010). © 2010 by C. Riddick Weber
TUNE: John Darwall (1770)

6.6.6.6.8.8.
DARWALL (342 D)

# Candle Glowing

# 63

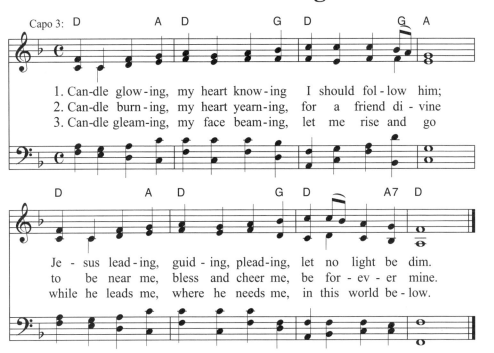

1. Can-dle glow-ing, my heart know-ing I should fol-low him;
2. Can-dle burn-ing, my heart yearn-ing, for a friend di-vine
3. Can-dle gleam-ing, my face beam-ing, let me rise and go

Je - sus lead-ing, guid - ing, plead-ing, let no light be dim.
to be near me, bless and cheer me, be for - ev - er mine.
while he leads me, where he needs me, in this world be - low.

4. Candle flaming, my heart naming
   Christ the Lord of all;
   Jesus, Savior, mine forever;
   I have heard your call.

5. Candle glorious - Christ victorious
   leads his people on
   into glory, forward journey,
   till the goal is won!

*On the last stanza, raise candles*

TEXT: Allen W. Schattschneider (1939), alt.
© 2013 by Interprovincial Board of Communication and
Moravian Music Foundation
TUNE: Melody, Johann Georg Hille (1739);
J. D. Grimm *Choralbuch* (1755); C. Gregor *Choralbuch* (1784)

8.5.8.5

SERVICE (56 A), first and last lines

# 64 We Humbly Gather in This Place

1. We humbly gather in this place to praise you, Lord, and seek your grace, and, Holy Spirit, we now pray: come, work among us ev-'ry day.

2. When human passions blind the mind, and fearfulness might rule the day, when on this earth no hope we find, be then our only hope and stay.

3. When all we've known must fade away, and all our joys dissolve to pain, when firm foundations turn to clay, we surely trust the Lamb once slain.

4. As we go forth to do your will, Lord, guide us, and your word fulfill, and show us how to work and be your blessed disciples, wholly free.

TEXT: St. 1, 4, John A. Craver (2006); st. 2,3, C. Daniel Crews.   L.M.
St. 1,4 © 2006 by John A. Craver; st. 2, 3 © 2013 by
Interprovincial Board of Communication and Moravian Music Foundation
TUNE: Thomas Tallis (1565)   TALLIS' CANON (22 T)

# Praise God This Special Day       65

1. Praise God this spe - cial day. Praise God for all the world. Praise
2. Bring peace, O God, bring peace to re - gions torn by war. Re -
3. Cre - ate new ways, O Lord. End need - less pain and strife. Bring
4. We come to you, O Lord, with songs of grat - i - tude, for

God for na - tions ev - 'ry - where with flags un - furled. Our prayers as -
lease the pow'r of un - der - stand - ing: hate no more. Our prayers as -
lead - ers to a com - mon ground; in - spire new life. Our prayers as -
all that you have giv - en us, our life, our food. Our prayers as -

cend for gov - ern - ments and lead - ers to up - hold God's will.
cend for sol - diers, youth, and cit - i - zens to seek your will.
cend for coun - cils and for trea - ties that pro - claim your will.
cend for this our na - tive land that it will choose your will.

TEXT: Willard R. Harstine (2004). © 2013 by Interprovincial Board of Communication       6.6.6.6.8.8.
    and Moravian Music Foundation
TUNE: John Darwall (1770)                                    DARWALL (342 D)

# 66     O Giver of These Years

1. O Giver of these years we claim as
ours to celebrate, remind us on this
banner day the challenge is still great.

2. O gracious God, whose love upholds your
people ev'rywhere, infuse us now with
eagerness your selfless way to share.

3. Revealer of the light that lifts the
darkness from our souls, rekindle now the
fire that fuels your church's long-sought goals.

4. O God of all the years we mark
as part of your broad plan,
inspire us as we now embark
on yet another span.

5. Enabler of your servant church,
equip us now, we pray,
for mission in the wider world,
beginning here today.

*Especially appropriate for
congregational anniversary celebrations.*

TEXT: Shirley Cox (1987). © 2013 by Interprovincial Board of Communication
and Moravian Music Foundation
TUNE: Este's *Psalter* (1592)

C.M

WINCHESTER, OLD (14 Z)

# Call to Worship

Moderato (♩ = 72)

We are here be-fore your pres-ence,_____ bow-ing
down_____ in hum - ble-ness,_____ giv-ing
ev - 'ry-thing we can_____ to you,_____ O_____
Lord._____ We are here,_____ bow-ing down___ be-fore the

TEXT: Jesmina Meade Hebbert (2009)
TUNE: Jesmina Meade Hebbert, arr. Nola Reed Knouse (2012)
Text and tune © 2013 Interprovincial Board of Communication and
Moravian Music Foundation.

Irregular
WE ARE HERE

# 68 Gather All Sisters and Brothers

1. Gath-er all sis-ters and broth-ers as one;
2. Gath-er in com-mu-ni-ty, pause to con-vey re-

join 'round the chal-ice: the cup of the Son.
freshed ded-i-ca-tion to Je-sus to-day.

Num-ber the bless-ings God's of-fered to you.
Drink from the grace-ful cup cov-e-nant wine,

An-swer with faith-ful-ness: your prom-ise re-new.
seal-ing your best in-tent, to live out God's de-sign.

*Especially appropriate for Cup of Covenant service*

TEXT: Christine Sobania Johnson (2003). © 2003 by Christine Sobania Johnson
TUNE: Traditional Irish melody

10.10.9.10
SLANE

# Bread of Life, for Others Broken  69

1. Bread of Life, for oth-ers bro-ken, cause us now to plain-ly see
2. Blood of Life, for oth-ers giv-en, shed for us, our glo-rious dress,

that those words for us were spo-ken: "Do this in my mem-o-ry."
shed that we might be for-giv-en, when sin-cere-ly we con-fess.

Yet, not on-ly in bread bro-ken, now re-mem-ber we the Son;
Yet, not on-ly this cup shar-ing, now re-mem-ber we the Son;

let our liv-ing be the to-ken that in Him we all are one.
may we too, for-giv-ing, car-ing, car-ry on what He has done.

*After 2nd verse*

Al-le-lu-ia, al-le-lu-ia, al-le-lu-ia, a - men!

TEXT: Samuel J. Gray (2000)
TUNE: Samuel J. Gray (2000)
© 2000 by Samuel J. Gray

8.7.8.7.D. with Alleluias
BREAD OF LIFE, NEW

# 70     **At the Passover With Jesus**

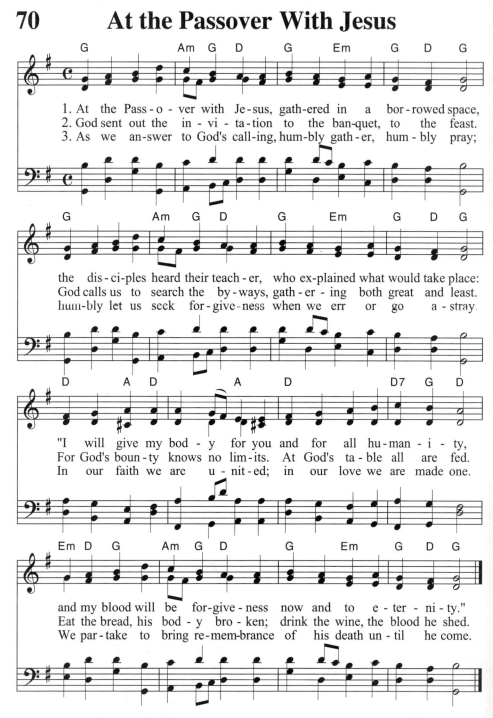

1. At the Pass-o-ver with Je-sus, gath-ered in a bor-rowed space,
2. God sent out the in-vi-ta-tion to the ban-quet, to the feast.
3. As we an-swer to God's call-ing, hum-bly gath-er, hum-bly pray;

the dis-ci-ples heard their teach-er, who ex-plained what would take place:
God calls us to search the by-ways, gath-er-ing both great and least.
hum-bly let us seek for-give-ness when we err or go a-stray.

"I will give my bod-y for you and for all hu-man-i-ty,
For God's boun-ty knows no lim-its. At God's ta-ble all are fed.
In our faith we are u-nit-ed; in our love we are made one.

and my blood will be for-give-ness now and to e-ter-ni-ty."
Eat the bread, his bod-y bro-ken; drink the wine, the blood he shed.
We par-take to bring re-mem-brance of his death un-til he come.

TEXT: St. 1, C. Riddick Weber (2011). © 2011 by C. Riddick Weber
    St. 2-3, June Edwards (2011), alt. © 2011 by June Edwards
TUNE: Herrnhut (c. 1735); C. Gregor *Choralbuch* (1784)

8.7.8.7.D. Trochaic

CASSEL (167 A)

# This Food

Moderato (♩ = 104-120)

1. This food is— good for my heart
food is— good for my heart,

—— and my bod - y. This food is so good for ev -'ry - one,
—— — my fam - 'ly. This food can— do — man-y things.

*Refrain*

—— — a par - ty! Come eat! Come be fit!— Com-
—— It's the life in you.

plete! So be it!—— Come eat! Come be fit!— Com-

plete! So be it!—— This food. This food. This food.

TEXT and MUSIC: David Melby-Gibbons (2012)

Irregular
THIS FOOD

# 72 Broken Man

**Andante** (♩ = 60)

Up-on the bro-ken man___ we place our-selves and our plans;_____ we come rush-ing back___ a - gain.

Up-on the bro-ken man___ we place our tired___ trem-bling hands,___

___ though we don't un - der-stand._____

TEXT and MUSIC: David Melby-Gibbons (2009).
  © 2013 Interprovincial Board of Communication and
  Moravian Music Foundation

Irreg
BROKEN M.

# Make the Lord's Love Known    73

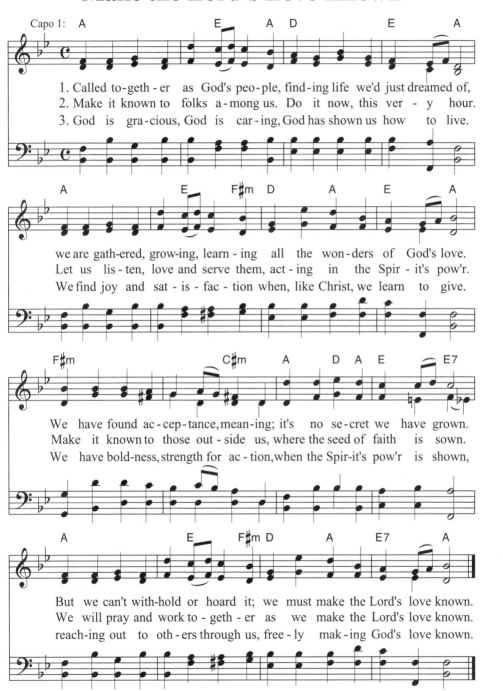

1. Called to-geth-er as God's peo-ple, find-ing life we'd just dreamed of,
2. Make it known to folks a-mong us. Do it now, this ver - y hour.
3. God is gra-cious, God is car-ing, God has shown us how to live.

we are gath-ered, grow-ing, learn-ing all the won-ders of God's love.
Let us lis-ten, love and serve them, act-ing in the Spir-it's pow'r.
We find joy and sat-is-fac-tion when, like Christ, we learn to give.

We have found ac-cep-tance, mean-ing; it's no se-cret we have grown.
Make it known to those out-side us, where the seed of faith is sown.
We have bold-ness, strength for ac-tion, when the Spir-it's pow'r is shown,

But we can't with-hold or hoard it; we must make the Lord's love known.
We will pray and work to-geth-er as we make the Lord's love known.
reach-ing out to oth-ers through us, free-ly mak-ing God's love known.

TEXT: Darryl Bell (1991, rev. 1993). © 1993 by Darryl Bell
TUNE: John Zundel (1870)

8.7.8.7.D. Trochaic
BEECHER (167 O)

# 74 Into the World

1. In-to the world Christ Je - sus sends us
2. In-to the world Christ Je - sus sends us
3. In-to the world Christ Je - sus sends us
4. In-to the world Christ Je - sus sends us

to speak his good news wher - ev - er we go:
to love like he loved wher - ev - er we go:
to make dis - ci - ples wher - ev - er we go:
to tell this mes - sage wher - ev - er we go:

"God's love is more than you'll i - mag - ine!
Just down the street, in - to the cit - ies,
Teach - ing his truth, seek - ing com - mit - ment,
"Life is for you! Now and for - ev - er!

TEXT: Christine Sobania Johnson (1999).
© 1999 by Christine Sobania Johnson
TUNE: Nola Reed Knouse (2000). © 2013 by Interprovincial Board of Communication
and Moravian Music Foundation

9.10.9.10.10.9

CHALLENGE

# 75 **Christian Workers**

1. Chris-tian work-ers, be de-ter-mined in the task at hand.
2. Chris-tian work-ers, give your tal-ents to the ho-ly plan.

Chris-tian broth-ers, Chris-tian sis-ters, yield to God's com-mand.
Feed the hun-gry, house the home-less, lend a help-ing hand.

May your life the Gos-pel prove, God on earth through faith can move.
Heal the sick, con-sole the weak; act through love, God's mes-sage speak.

Chris-tian work-ers, be com-mit-ted to God's min-is-try.
Chris-tian work-ers, be com-mit-ted to God's min-is-try.

TEXT: Nancy Morgan (1987). © 1987 by Nancy Morgan.
TUNE: Melody, Johann Georg Hille (1739); Johann Daniel Grimm *Choralbuch* (1755);
C. Gregor *Choralbuch* (1784)

8.5.8.5.7.7.8.5.
SERVICE (56 A)

# Come, Be With Our Friend Jesus 76

1. Come, be with our friend Je - sus, our God in hu-man form,
2. Let us with all cre - a - tion now dance and cel - e - brate.

who came to earth to save__ us, and to make love the norm.
God wants you at the par - ty, so please don't hes - i - tate.

He guides us by the Spir - it, and leads us on our way,
For this is where all peo - ple will join and sing one song.

to__ be a place of safe - ty, and wel - come ev -'ry day.
All__ wel-come in one fam - 'ly, to know that all be - long.

TEXT: Hymn-writing workshop participants, Moravian Theological Seminary (2009).
   © 2013 by Interprovincial Board of Communication and
   Moravian Music Foundation
TUNE: Melchior Teschner (1613); C. Gregor *Choralbuch* (1784)

7.6.7.6.D.

ST. THEODULPH (151 G)

MISSION
**77**

# Hope in the Wilderness
## (Amazing Grace, How Can It Be)

1. A - maz - ing grace, how can it be that God to us is true,
2. That love in-spired the ear-ly church to reach out to the slaves,
3. We're called to take the risk-y step, a - lign with those in need,

that we are pre-cious in God's sight, de - spite the things we do?
to ven-ture in - to un - known lands and chal-lenge un - just ways.
to vis-ion the new thing God's doing with-in com - mu - ni - ty.

Cre - a - tor, form-er, shap-er, mak-ing real what we have known,
In wil - der - ness of pov - er - ty, of harsh-ness, pain, and death;
The chal-lenge is to not re - ly on raw re - al - i - ty

that God's love is de - pend - a - ble, and names us as God's own.
a new thing was made pos - si - ble by liv - ing out one's faith.
that shrouds our hope, ob - scur - ing all that God would have us see.

*May also be sung to KINGSFOLD, MBW 524, or FOREST GREEN, MBW481.*

TEXT: Judith M. Ganz (2007). © 2007 by Judith M. Ganz
TUNE: Johann Crüger (1649)

C.M.D.
ST. SIMON (590 C)

4. This wilderness is filled with hate, with violence and pain,
   as vengeance-seeking, market gain, and gross injustice reign.
   But as we join those most oppressed, and face the mess we see;
   the river flows -- God in our midst, the joy that sets us free.

5. That river flows for all the world, and as God's own we are
   the means for grace and love to heal the wounds and mend the scars.
   God's love that stirred our church back then, still moves our church today,
   Creator, former, shaper, bringing new, transforming ways.

# As Twig Is Bent, So Grows the Tree    78

TEXT: John D. Rights (2009). © 2009 by Mary White Rights
TUNE: *Cantionale Germanicum* (1628); C. Gregor *Choralbuch* (1784)

L.M.
HUS (22 F)

# 79 Let Us Follow Our Lamb

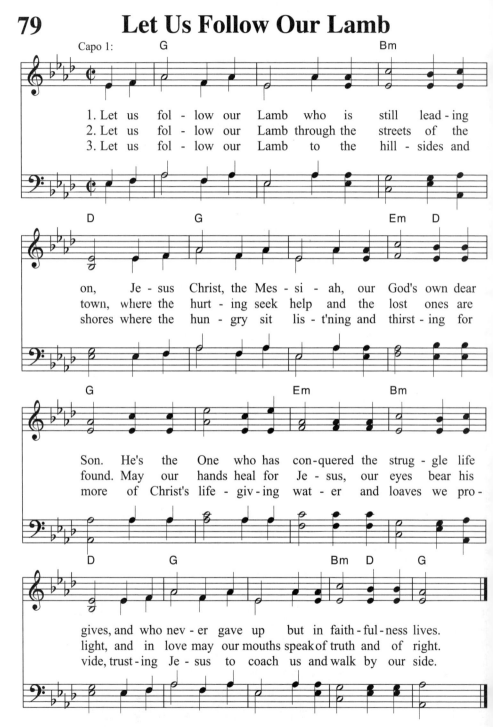

Capo 1:

1. Let us fol - low our Lamb who is still lead - ing
2. Let us fol - low our Lamb through the streets of the
3. Let us fol - low our Lamb to the hill - sides and

on, Je - sus Christ, the Mes - si - ah, our God's own dear
town, where the hurt - ing seek help and the lost ones are
shores where the hun - gry sit lis - t'ning and thirst - ing for

Son. He's the One who has con - quered the strug - gle life
found. May our hands heal for Je - sus, our eyes bear his
more of Christ's life - giv - ing wat - er and loaves we pro -

gives, and who nev - er gave up but in faith - ful - ness lives.
light, and in love may our mouths speak of truth and of right.
vide, trust - ing Je - sus to coach us and walk by our side.

TEXT: Sharon Michel Benson (2010). © 2010 by Sharon Michel Benson
TUNE: J. Funk's *A Compilation of Genuine Church Music* (1832).
    Harm. Margaret S. Kortz (1967)

11.11.11.11.
FOUNDATION (39 H)

4.  Let us follow our Lamb through the doors of the church
    where we pray, worship, study with those who would search
    for our Lamb's words and wisdom, his courage and grace.
    May we love one another in such sacred space.

5.  Let us follow our Lamb even up Calv'ry's rise
    knowing nothing can stop God's great plan for our lives,
    for his tomb is still empty, and ours will be too.
    As we faithfully follow he conquers anew.

# Praying with Paul (An Apology)   80

I think it'd be cool to speak in the tongues of men and angels.
*You gave me no water for my feet ...*

**O Lord of the long and winding road; the high places; the narrow path and the valley of the shadow of death, have mercy on me. May the great and wondrous gifts I seek be found in humble acts that refresh the weary and heavy-laden.**

I want the gift of prophecy and to be able to fathom all mysteries and all knowledge, and have a faith that can move mountains.
*You gave me no kiss ...*

**O Holy One of sorrows; despised and acquainted with grief, I am sorry. May all the wisdom I need be gained through a loving embrace of the lonely, the lost, and the least.**

I may consider giving all I possess to the poor but can't even imagine surrendering my body to the flames.
*You did not anoint my head with oil ...*

**O Child of the Manger and God of the Cross, please forgive. May the sacrifice of wealth and works in which we trust never displace the obedience and intimacy you desire. May my tithes and offerings ever be the first and best of justice, mercy, and faithfulness.**

Emmanuel, God with us, Living Word in our midst ...
Grant that we may:
**Seek your Kingdom before all else**
**Honor you above all else**
**Love more than all else**
**Amen.**

© by Brian Dixon

# 81 Visions of Glory

1. Vi - sions of glo - ry, vi - sions tri - um - phant, bright won - ders
2. Still, Lord, too of - ten we miss your vi - sion; that we have
3. Help us to bal - ance all of our choic - es; help us to

dance, Lord, charm-ing our eyes; yet, Lord, you call us to hum - ble
failed you we must con-fess: we con-fuse ser - vice with our am -
look both for - ward and back; help us to hear you in all your

ser - vice, do - ing your will, Lord, in the real world.
bi - tion; on - ly your lead - ing brings true suc - cess.
voic - es which sing the wis - dom our voic - es lack.

TEXT: C. Daniel Crews (1999). © 2013 by Interprovincial Board of Communication
    and Moravian Music Foundation
TUNE: Gaelic melody. Setting © 1993 by Brian Henkelmann

5.5.5.4.D

BUNESSAN

# Lord, You Give Beyond All Measure 82

1. Lord, you give be-yond all meas-ure: gifts of beau-ty, gifts of grace,
2. We are called to faith-ful ser-vice for the bless-ings from your hand,
3. Lord, I of-fer but a por-tion what you have on me be-stowed.

gifts of earth and gifts of heav-en, gifts for all the hu-man race;
to re-turn the gifts you've grant-ed, stew-ards in your per-fect plan.
Seal my heart; make me an of-f'ring, for-ward in Christ's way I go.

sa-cred gift of Christ, most bless-ed, free-dom from our sins con-fess-ed:
Free us from our earth-ly treas-ure; us u-nite in heav'n-ly pleas-ure.
I com-mit my time and treas-'ry: tal-ent, skill with which you've blessed me.

all we have comes from a-bove. Thank you, Lord, for bound-less love.
May we sense from heav'n a-bove how to live out Bound-less Love.
I re-turn to you a-bove gifts re-ceived:your bound-less love.

TEXT: Nancy Sawtelle (2007). © 2007 by Nancy Sawtelle
TUNE: Christoph Anton (c. 1642); C. Gregor *Choralbuch* (1784)

8.7.8.7.8.8.7.7. Trochaic
ZURICH (168 A)

# 83    Love of God Is a Fragrant Garden

1. Love of God is a fra - grant__ gar - den, full of col - or,__ life and fruit. Through - out its an - nual cy - cle, we find seed and bulb and shoot.
2. Sci - ence teach - es us all life's__ cy - cles; faith__ turns them in - to song: to - geth - er__ they can guide us through - out our__ whole lives long.
3. We__ cel - e - brate Co - me - nius as the teach-er we know the best. Still__ more en - larged his__ wis - dom e - ven though we__ know them less:
4. Like__ them let us praise our Cre - a - tor and re - joice in__ God's lar - gesse, of - fer thanks un - to the__ Sav - ior, who en - dured cre - a - tion's dis - tress,

TEXT: C. Riddick Weber (2011). © 2011 by C. Riddick Weber
TUNE: Irish folksong. Harmonization by Nola Reed Knouse (2012).
    © 2013 by Interprovincial Board of Communication
    and Moravian Music Foundation

9.7.7.7.8.6.8.6.
SALLEY GARDENS

Hid - ing un - der the snows of win - ter, soak - ing
With hum - ble thanks we learn to see what
Broth - er Da - vid and Bish - op George, Sis - ter
and sing now to the Spir - it, whose

up the rain of spring, bath - ing in the gold of
those be - fore us saw: com - pre - hend - ing God's cre -
An - na in the wood, fur - thered what we know of
gifts be - yond com - pare en - a - ble us God's

sum - mer, they an au - tumn har - vest bring.
a - tion in - stills a great - er awe.
na - ture and shared that as they could.
bless - ings to stu - dy, reap and share.

John Amos Comenius (1592-1670), Bishop of the *Unitas Fratrum*, has been called the "Father of Modern Education."

Brother David refers to Lewis David de Schweinitz, the first American to earn a Ph.D. In addition to being the father of mycology, he was also an ordained Moravian pastor, administrator, and educator.

Bishop George refers to George Higgins, Moravian bishop, who was active in Christian education and in the camping ministries of Laurel Ridge Camp and Conference Center, in addition to his renowned knowledge of the flora and fauna on and around the North Carolina mountains.

Sister Anna refers to Anna Rosina Gambold (d. 1821), who served as a missionary among the Cherokee in northwest Georgia prior to the Trail of Tears. She was renowned for her vast botanical knowledge.

# 84 God, the Lord of All Creation

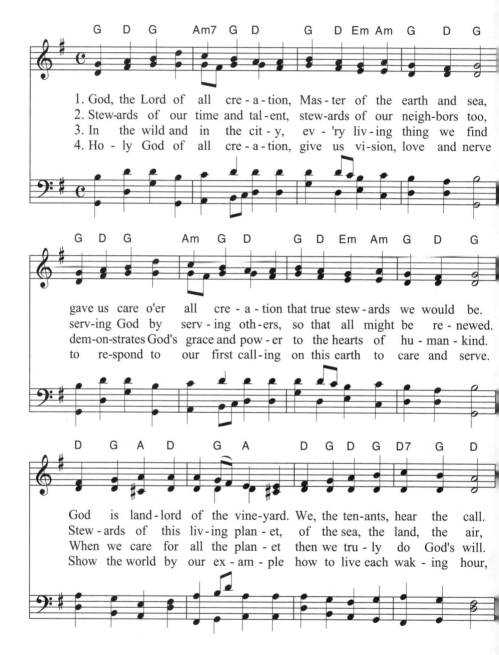

1. God, the Lord of all cre-a-tion, Mas-ter of the earth and sea,
2. Stew-ards of our time and tal-ent, stew-ards of our neigh-bors too,
3. In the wild and in the cit-y, ev-'ry liv-ing thing we find
4. Ho-ly God of all cre-a-tion, give us vi-sion, love and nerve

gave us care o'er all cre-a-tion that true stew-ards we would be.
serv-ing God by serv-ing oth-ers, so that all might be re-newed.
dem-on-strates God's grace and pow-er to the hearts of hu-man-kind.
to re-spond to our first call-ing on this earth to care and serve.

God is land-lord of the vine-yard. We, the ten-ants, hear the call.
Stew-ards of this liv-ing plan-et, of the sea, the land, the air,
When we care for all the plan-et then we tru-ly do God's will.
Show the world by our ex-am-ple how to live each wak-ing hour,

TEXT: St. 1-3, June Edwards. © 2012 by June Edwards
    St. 4, Rick Beck. © 2013 by Interprovincial Board of Communication
    and Moravian Music Foundation
TUNE: Herrnhut (c. 1735); C. Gregor *Choralbuch* (1784)

8.7.8.7.D. Trochaic

CASSEL (167 A)

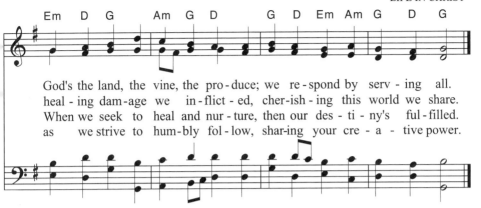

God's the land, the vine, the pro-duce; we re-spond by serv-ing all.
heal-ing dam-age we in-flict-ed, cher-ish-ing this world we share.
When we seek to heal and nur-ture, then our des-ti-ny's ful-filled.
as we strive to hum-bly fol-low, shar-ing your cre-a-tive power.

## The Echo of Love 85

I suppose worship to be the heartbeat of faith.
Which is not to say that it is the *heart* of faith.

No, worship is not that vital organ: the pressure behind,
the force within; reservoir and wellspring of our life
and the living of it.

I think that would be God.

And, neither is to say that worship is the heartbeat of faith
To say that it is the *lifeblood* of faith.

No, worship is not that precious flow which fills and floods;
Current and conveyance of warmth and heat and strength.

I think that would be the Holy Spirit.

Nor can worship properly be said to be the *body*
Throughout and through which the heart and blood of faith move:
Raising bones to new life and light in the darkness,
Lifting up the wounded and the broken
And walking with them.

I think that would be Christ Jesus
And the Church through which He lives.

Leaving worship to be the echo of love,
Re-citing, Re-sounding, Breathing again
The rhythm and pulse of our dancing days with God.

# 86 We Are God's People

**Lively (♩ = c. 104)**

1. We are God's peo - ple, the ones God re - deems.___
2. We need the for - ests to breathe, yes, we do.___
3. We love the sun - shine, but we need the rain to
4. Stu - dents and teach - ers, we learn side by side; in

We are God's peo - ple;___ God gives us dreams to
We need the o - ceans; they help the world too. To
bring us the flow - ers, the mud, and the grain. And
self - less com - pas - sion our work's dig - ni - fied. The

TEXT: Rebecca Rominger and Robert Rominger (2008)
TUNE: Robert Rominger with Rebecca Rominger (2008)
©2008 by Rebecca L. Rominger and Robert L. Rominger III

Irregular
GOD'S PEOPLE

make    the    world    bet - ter    by    op - 'ning    our    hands    to
make    the    dream    hap - pen⏤    we    need    to    start    by
when    the    fog's    lift - ed    we'll    see    clear    to    find    the
world    is    our    class - room:    let's    treat    it    with    care    as

care    for    each    oth - er    and    clean    up    the    land.
lead - ing    the    peo - ple⏤    in - to    God's    heart.
treas - ure    we    lost    when    the    clouds    made    us    blind.
we    read    the    les - sons    God    leaves    for    us    there.

*Last time*

# 87 Won't You Walk with Me, Jesus

1. Won't you walk with me, Je-sus, down the long road of life? Won't you
2. Won't you guide me, my Je-sus, when I don't know the way? Won't you
3. Won't you laugh with me, Je-sus, when my heart's full of joy? Won't you
4. Won't you sing with me, Je-sus, won't you sing my new song? Won't you
5. Won't you walk with me, Je-sus, down the long road of life? Won't you

walk with me, Je - sus, all the way?
guide me, my Je - sus, on my way?
laugh with me, Je - sus, in my joy?
sing with me, Je - sus, sing a - long?
walk with me, Je - sus, all the way?

TEXT and MUSIC David M. Henkelmann (1971).
© 2013 by Interprovincial Board of Communication
and Moravian Music Foundation

7.6.7.3.with Refra
WALK WITH ME JESU

*Refrain*

D    D7    Em    E7

I keep see-ing you in oth-ers, in my sis-ters, in my broth-ers; help me

D    Em7    A7    D

reach out, O Je - sus, on my way.

# 88 As You Once Called Two Brothers

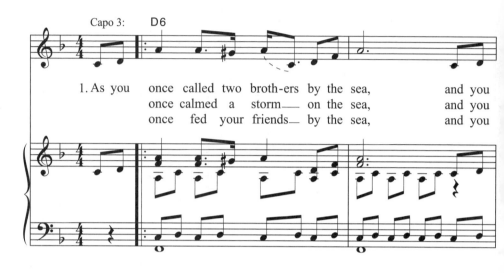

1. As you once called two broth-ers by the sea, and you
once calmed a storm on the sea, and you
once fed your friends by the sea, and you

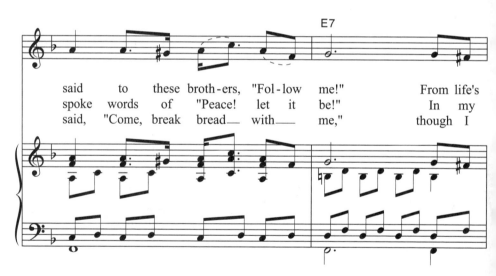

said to these broth-ers, "Fol-low me!" From life's
spoke words of "Peace! let it be!" In my
said, "Come, break bread with me," though I

TEXT and MUSIC: David M Henkelmann (1981).
© 2013 by Interprovincial Board of Communication and
Moravian Music Foundation

10.10.6.6.9.
CALL ME

hus - tle and roar we have come to this shore. When you're
ra - ging and doubt, fears with - in and with - out, as you
eat my full share, still a hun - ger is there. I need

call - ing to oth-ers, call me. 2. As you
once calmed that storm, calm me. 3. As you
more, O my Lord, feed me.

# Jesus, Still Lead On

**89**

**Spirito (♩ = 100-112)**

Je - sus, still lead on till __ our rest be won, and __ al - though the way be cheer-less,

(when) we seek re - lief from a long-felt grief, when __ temp - ta - tions come al - lur - ing,

TEXT: Nicholas Ludwig von Zinzendorf (1721);
    recast Christian Gregor (1778). Tr. Jane L. Borthwick (1846), alt.
TUNE: Steve Gray (2010). © 2010 by Steve Gray

5.5.8.8.5.5

LEAD O

we  will  fol - low, calm and fear - less; guide us by your hand  to____
make  us  pa - tient and en - dur - ing; show us that bright shore where

____ the prom - ised  land.  Je  -  sus, still lead on,___ lead  on.
____ we weep no  more.  Je  -  sus, still lead on,___ lead  on.

If ____ the  way  be  drear,  if __
Je  -  sus, still lead  on ____  till

# 90 I Search for You, Lord

Moderato (♩ = 104)

1. I search for you, Lord, in the wash-ing and churn-ing of o-cean's tide. I look for your pres-ence in all of the bright-ness of morn-ing's sky.

stand in the cit-y and no-tice the peo-ple who live and die. I look in their fac-es and see the noth-ing of years gone by.

Lord, I won-der in all that is, and will pow-er of love and peace be known to hu-man-kind?

TEXT and TUNE: Rick Sides and Jim Newsom, Jr. (1974)
© 2013 Interprovincial Board of Communication and
Moravian Music Foundation

Irregular
I SEARCH FOR YOU, LORD

I wan - der in fields___ of clo-ver and flow-ers that
I weep for the heart - ache and all of the dreams that are
Will o - ceans and skies___ and fields and flow - ers

smell so sweet._____ I feel___ the brown earth and
shat - tered here._____ I feel the dark shad - ows, the
ev - er know_____ that we___ are here___ be -

soft grass un - der my feet.
lone - li - ness and the fear.
cause you love___ us so?

Lord,_____ I

LIFE IN CHRIST

# 91 God, Your Love Brought Forth Creation

1. God, your love brought forth cre - a - tion, raised from death the
2. Made to live at one with oth - ers, we build hu - man
3. Christ, who lev - eled walls and la - bels, wants a church that's
4. Cen - turies old, God's church is __ liv - ing with a fu - ture

Cru - ci - fied; now you're liv - ing with us, __ call - ing
bar - riers high; we make la - bels to di - vide us;
bar - rier - free, where all peo - ple are made wel - come
that's un - known: threat and prom - ise both be - fore us,

us to live like Christ who died. Lord, a - mong us you are
born to live, we choose to __ die. Yet, a - mong us God is
with a grace that all can see. We through grace are all God's
we are God's and not our own. God, you call us; make us

TEXT: Hermann I. Weinlick (1986). © 2013 by Interprovincial Board of Communication and
Moravian Music Foundation
TUNE: Traditional French melody

8.7.8.7.8.7.

PICARDY

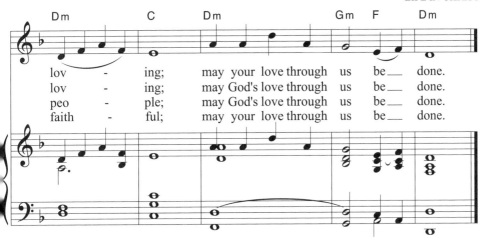

| | lov | - | ing; | may your love through | us | be — | done. |
| | lov | - | ing; | may God's love through | us | be — | done. |
| | peo | - | ple; | may God's love through | us | be — | done. |
| | faith | - | ful; | may your love through | us | be — | done. |

# For Us and Of Us          92

When we were not a people

**Love made us one.**

When we were without help or hope in the world

**Love made us one.**

When there was no place we could call "home"

**Love made us one.**
**A people of Love**
**And, for others**
**Help and hope for the life of the world**
**Where Love's weary and burdened children**
**Come to a place of rest.**

For us and of us

**The Beloved Son is building His Church.**

For us and of us

**The Spirit of Truth is raising the Temple.**

For us and of us

**Unending Love has made a home.**
**Amen.**

© by Brian Dixon

# 93 As God's Beloved and Chosen Ones

Capo 1: D      A   Bm   G    A    D

1. As God's be-lov'd and cho-sen ones, we an-swer then your
2. We bear an-oth-er's bur-dens, Lord, for-giv-ing and for-
3. Your love and peace will rule our hearts; u-nite us in-to
4. With wis-dom and a grate-ful heart we sing our psalms of

A      D   G     Em     A

call to clothe in self-hu-mil-i-ty, com-
giv'n. You clothe us in your per-fect love, as
one. Your word dwells rich-ly in our souls, our
praise. The hymns, that nur-tured faith, re-new our

Bm    G      A          D

pas-sion, meek-ness, pa-tience, love. In the name of Je-sus
pure as har-mo-ny a-bove. In the name of Je-sus
thank-ful-ness to you o'er-flows. In the name of Je-sus,
words and deeds and all we do in the name of Je-sus.

TEXT: Barbara Strauss (1995), based on Col. 3:12-17.
© 1995 by Barbara Strauss
TUNE: C. Hubert H. Parry (1888)

8.6.8.8.7.6.

REPTON

live:            so    oth - ers    we        for - give.
live:            our   love   to    oth  -  ers  give.
where            his   wis - dom    we        can  share.
Praise:          our   grate - ful  songs     we   raise.

## We Thank You With Singing    94

We thank you with sing-ing, we thank you with voice; we thank you with

ac-tions; we make this our choice. Our mon-ey, our ser-vice, our

tal-ents, our all__ we give to you glad-ly__to an-swer your call!

TEXT: Christine Sobania Johnson (2004).
   © 2004 by Christine Sobania Johnson
TUNE: Herrnhut (c. 1740); C. Gregor *Choralbuch* (1784)

11.11.11.11. Anapestic

CONFESSION (39 A)

**95** **Refreshed by Living Waters**

Re-freshed by liv-ing wa-ters, re-newed by liv-ing bread,
may we, your sons and daugh-ters, by your own hand be led.
Ac-cept the gifts we of-fer, re-ceive the lives we owe,
u-nite us in your ser-vice, may deeds of mer-cy grow.

TEXT: Nancy Morgan (2000). © 2000 by Nancy Morgan
TUNE: Samuel Sebastian Wesley (1864)

7.6.7.6.D.
AURELIA (151 L)

# Benediction

1. In the name of the Fa - ther, and of the Son,
2. In the name of the Fa - ther, and of the Son,

and of the Ho - ly Spir - it, go now in faith, go now in hope,
and of the Ho - ly Spir - it, a - men, a - men,

go now in peace, go forth in love.
a - men, a - men.

TEXTand TUNE: Brad Bennett (2007)
© 2007 by Brad Bennett

BENEDICTION

# FESTIVALS OF THE CHRISTIAN CHURCH
# AND MEMORIAL DAYS OF THE UNITAS FRATRUM

## Immovable Festivals

| | |
|---|---|
| December 25 | Christmas: the nativity of our Lord. |
| January 6 | Epiphany, or the manifestation of Christ to the Gentiles. |
| January 19 | Beginning of the mission work of the Unitas Fratrum in Greenland (1733) |
| February 2 | Presentation of Christ in the temple |
| March 1 | Founding of the Unitas Fratrum (March 1) |
| March 25 | The Annunciation; Festival of all the Choirs |
| April 30 | Day of Prayer and Covenanting for Widows |
| May 4 | Day of Prayer and Covenanting for Single Sisters |
| May 12 | Adoption of the Brotherly Agreement and Statutes (Covenant for Christian Living) at Herrnhut, 1727 |
| June 4 | Day of Prayer and Covenanting for Older Girls |
| June 17 | Beginning of Herrnhut by emigrants from Moravia (1722) |
| July 6 | Martyrdom of John Hus (1415) |
| July 9 | Day of Prayer and Covenanting for Older Boys (alternate, October 21) |
| August 13 | Spiritual renewal of the Unitas Fratrum at Herrnhut (1722) |
| August 17 | Day of Prayer and Covenanting for Children |
| August 21 | Beginning of Moravian missions (1732) |
| August 29 | Day of Prayer and Covenanting for Single Brethren |
| August 31 | Day of Prayer and Covenanting for Widowers |
| September 7 | Day of Prayer and Covenanting for Married Brethren and Sisters |
| September 16 | Day of Prayer and Covenanting for ministers of the Unitas Fratrum, commemorating a powerful experience (1741) of the fact that Jesus Christ is the Chief Elder of his church (see November 13) |
| September 29 | (St. Michael and All Angels); Memorial Day for all who are engaged in the instruction of children and youth |
| October 31 | Beginning of the German Reformation (1517) |
| November 1 | All Saints Day |
| November 13 | Formal acknowledgment that Jesus Christ is the Chief Elder of his church (1741; see September 16) |

## Movable Festivals

Advent begins on the Sunday nearest November 30 (St. Andrew's Day), whether before or after.

Easter is always the first Sunday after the full moon on or next after March 21; if the full moon happens on Sunday, Easter is the Sunday after.

Ash Wednesday, on which Lent begins, is 46 days before Easter.

Ascension Day is 40 days after Easter. Pentecost is 7 weeks after Easter.

Trinity Sunday is 8 weeks after Easter.

| Year | Ash Wed. | Easter Sunday | Year | Ash Wed. | Easter Sunday | Year | Ash Wed. | Easter Sunday | Year | Ash Wed. | Easter Sunday |
|---|---|---|---|---|---|---|---|---|---|---|---|
| 2013 | Feb. 13 | Mar. 31 | 2017 | Mar. 1 | Apr. 16 | 2021 | Feb. 17 | Apr. 4 | 2025 | Mar. 5 | Apr. 20 |
| 2014 | Mar. 5 | Apr. 20 | 2018 | Feb. 14 | Apr. 1 | 2022 | Mar. 2 | Apr. 17 | 2026 | Feb. 18 | Apr. 5 |
| 2015 | Feb. 18 | Apr. 5 | 2019 | Mar. 6 | Apr. 21 | 2023 | Feb. 22 | Apr. 9 | 2027 | Feb. 10 | Mar. 28 |
| 2016 | Feb. 10 | Mar. 27 | 2020 | Feb. 26 | Apr. 12 | 2024 | Feb. 14 | Mar. 31 | 2028 | Mar. 1 | Apr. 16 |

# ADDRESSES OF COPYRIGHT HOLDERS

The addresses of copyright holders with four or more items in this publication are listed below. Other addresses are given in the acknowledgments which follow.

RICK BECK, 122 Rocky Ridge Point, NW, Calgary, Alberta, T3G 4R5 Canada
BRIAN DIXON, 7440 Victoria Drive, Victoria, MN 55386
SAMUEL J. GRAY, 6910 Kenbridge Dr., Clemmons, NC 27012
STEVE GRAY, 540 Rabbit Farm Trail, Advance, NC 27006
IBOC (INTERPROVINCIAL BOARD OF COMMUNICATION), 1021 Center St., Bethlehem, PA 18018
CHRISTINE SOBANIA JOHNSON, PO Box 327 Gnadenhutten, OH 44629
MMF (MORAVIAN MUSIC FOUNDATION), 457 S. Church Street, Winston-Salem, NC 27101
ROBERT L. ROMINGER, III, 2850 Deerwood Dr., Winston-Salem, NC 27103

| | | | |
|---|---|---|---|
| 1 | Hymn stanza, text © IBOC and MMF | 43 | Music © IBOC and MMF; text © Erdmute Frank, August-Bebel-Strasse 4, 02747 Herrnhut, Germany |
| 2 | Text and music © Steve Gray | | |
| 4 | Text © Christine Sobania Johnson | | |
| 9 | Text © John Craver, 4012 Apperson Rd., East Bend, NC 27018 | 44 | Text © IBOC and MMF |
| | | 45 | Text © Susan Cox Starbuck, 2225 Westfield Ave., Winston-Salem, NC 27103 |
| 16 | Text © Brian Dixon | | |
| 17 | Text © IBOC and MMF | 46 | Text and music © IBOC and MMF |
| 18 | Text © IBOC and MMF | 47 | Music © Samuel J. Gray |
| 19 | Text © M. Lynnette Delbridge, 1646 Victory Blvd., Staten Island, NY 10314 | 48 | Text and music © Robert L. Rominger, III |
| | | 49 | Text and music © IBOC and MMF |
| 20 | Text © IBOC and MMF | 50 | Harmonization © Steve Gray and Samuel J. Gray |
| 22 | Music © Steve Gray | | |
| 23 | Text © Robert L. Rominger, III | 51 | Text and music © Paul Schick, 507 W. Wilson St., Apt. 307, Madison, WI 53703 |
| 24 | Text and music © Zachariah D. Bailey, 40 E. Second Ave, Lititz, PA 17543 | | |
| | | 52 | Text © IBOC and MMF |
| 25 | Text © IBOC and MMF | 53 | Music © IBOC and MMF; text © Barbara Prillaman, 1316 Rothes Dr., Cary, NC 27511 |
| 26 | Text © IBOC and MMF | | |
| 27 | Text © Gilbert Frank, 3238 Polo Rd., Winston-Salem, NC 27106 | | |
| | | 54 | Text © Mary White Rights, 3428 Luther St., Winston-Salem, NC 27127 |
| 28 | Text © IBOC and MMF | | |
| 29 | Text © Gilbert Frank, 3238 Polo Rd., Winston-Salem, NC 27106 | 55 | Text © Thom Stapleton, Thom.Stapleton@moravian.org.uk |
| 30 | Text and music © Dirk French, P.O. Box 778, Davidson, NC 28036 | 56 | Text © IBOC and MMF |
| | | 57 | Text and music © Brad Bennett, 395 Janet Ave., Winston-Salem, NC 27104 |
| 31 | Text © IBOC and MMF | | |
| 32 | Text © IBOC and MMF | 58 | Text © IBOC and MMF |
| 33 | Text © IBOC and MMF | 59 | Text © IBOC and MMF |
| 34 | Text and music © Jill B. Bruckart, 408 Bridgeboro St., Riverside, NJ 08075 | 60 | Text © Barbara J. Strauss, 1989 W. 58th St., Cleveland, OH 44102 |
| 35 | Text and music © 1990 Steve Gray | 61 | Text and music © IBOC and MMF |
| 36 | Text © Christine Sobania Johnson | 62 | Text © C. Riddick Weber, 120 Cross Gate Court, Winston-Salem, NC 27106 |
| 37 | Text and music © IBOC and MMF | | |
| 38 | Text © Richard L. Bruckart, 408 Bridgeboro St., Riverside, NJ 08075 | 63 | Text © IBOC and MMF |
| | | 64 | Text verses 1, 4 © John Craver, 4012 Apperson Rd., East Bend, NC 27018; verses 2, 3 © IBOC and MMF |
| 39 | Text and music © Robert L. Rominger, III | | |
| 40 | Text © Christine Sobania Johnson | | |
| 41 | Text © Brian Dixon | 65 | Text © IBOC and MMF |
| 42 | Text and music © IBOC and MMF | 66 | Text © IBOC and MMF |

# COMPOSERS, ARRANGERS, AUTHORS, TRANSLATORS, AND SOURCES

# SEASONAL AND TOPICAL INDEX

# BIBLICAL REFERENCES AND ALLUSIONS

# ALPHABETICAL INDEX OF FIRST LINES